LEISURE CYCLING NEAR DUBLIN

Hugh Halpin

Gill & Macmillan

Gill & Macmillan Ltd
Hume Avenue, Park West, Dublin 12
with associated companies throughout the world
www.gillmacmillan.ie
© Hugh Halpin 2006
ISBN-13: 978 07171 4005 3
ISBN-10: 0 7171 4005 9
Design and print origination by Carole Lynch
Maps by EastWest Mapping, Clonegal, Enniscorthy, Co. Wexford
Printed and bound by Nørhaven Paperback A/S, Denmark

This book is typeset in 9pt Sabon on 11pt.

*The paper used in this book comes from the wood pulp of
managed forests. For every tree felled, at least one tree
is planted, thereby renewing natural resources.*

The author and publishers have taken every care to ensure that the
information contained in this book is accurate at the time of writing.
In the nature of the subject, however, changes can and do occur. The
author and publishers shall have no liability in respect of any loss or
damage, however caused, arising out of the use of this guide. This
includes — but is not limited to — loss or damage resulting from missing
signs, future changes in routes, accidents and lost or injured persons.

A CIP catalogue record for this book is available
from the British Library.

1 3 5 4 2

Contents

Contents

Acknowledgments

A project like this cannot be completed without the support of many. I would like to thank Aine for allowing me to invade her space with masses of clutter. My thanks also go to those who gave me information, direction and encouragement, especially during the faltering times. Finally, the loneliness of my long-distance cycling was relieved by those who cycled with me, and especially Pat Noone whose regular company was inspirational.

INTRODUCTION TO ROUTES

Leisure Cycling Near Dublin is a book for both cyclists or would-be cyclists to enjoy, comprising 40 1-day cycling routes near the City. The focus is on enjoying the countryside in a leisurely fashion and taking time to explore, and there is no better way to explore the byways of the region than by bicycle. The book will guide you through spectacular countryside to wonderful places of interest, some well off the beaten track. The routes are purposely selected to avoid busy roads, yet each is about an hour's drive or less from Dublin City. For convenience, all the routes are circuits enabling the cyclist to start and finish at the same place, making it easier to pick up a car or public transport. Also the estimated time for each route is provided, along with the distance from the City centre to the start; this will facilitate planning the day. Replenishment is seldom an issue, with plenty of towns and villages on most routes.

The countryside and terrain are varied, with easy cycling along the plains of Kildare through to the more challenging routes in the mountains of Wicklow. As well as Kildare and Wicklow, the routes traverse counties Dublin, Fingal, Meath and Louth, and even a little of some outer counties. These too provide a wealth of varied and interesting cycles. If you have not been cycling for a while you could start with the easy, shorter routes to build your fitness level, before trying the more difficult and longer ones. The main purpose should be to enjoy the cycling, as taking on too much too quickly can be discouraging. However, if you are an experienced cyclist, then the more challenging terrains may be for you. Each route is classed under four terrain types: flat, rolling, hilly and mountainous. The routes vary between 20 and 95 km, the longer ones are good for those who are fit and want to stretch themselves. But whatever your level there are routes to suit you.

If your interest is heritage, then you will not be disappointed. The region is abundant, and the many churches, castles and mansions are reminders of romantic and turbulent times, of saints and scholars, invading armies and powerful lords. Meath is particularly rich in heritage and the Valley of Kings route, for example, is filled with myth and history scattered along the beautiful Boyne Valley on a mere 30-km cycle. But even the most remote route has something to offer.

Backgrounds to the historic sites visited are provided in the route descriptions.

For nature lovers, the routes provide a range of habitats, from coast to bog and mountain to plain. The pace allows the cyclist to catch movements of foraging animals, and hear the multitude of birdsong. It is advisable to carry binoculars if you wish to take full advantage of the fauna. For flora lovers too, many of the fine houses to be visited possess beautiful gardens such as Powerscourt on the Glencree route. The Curragh route includes the unique Japanese Gardens, and Pollardstown Fen is a special wildlife habitat of international importance.

Finally, if a route is not convenient to your location then it will be necessary to use private or public transport to get to the start. For driving, the book gives directions and parking facilities for each route start, as well as general information on carrying bicycles on vehicles. Public transport is not always convenient; however, the companies that provide a bicycle-carrying service are listed under 'Transporting Bicycles' along with contact numbers.

ROUTE SUMMARIES

At the beginning of each route a summary table is given to indicate the characteristics of the route. Included in the table are:

Distance: the approximate distance in kilometres to complete a route, including detours.

Time: the approximate time to complete a route at a leisurely pace and based on regular short stops. It does not include long periods at local sights e.g. taking a local tour of a castle or gardens.

Terrain gives an indication of route gradients. There are four classes:

Flat <50 m and may be regarded as easy cycling.

Rolling <100 m

Hilly <200 m

Mountainous >200 m and may be regarded as challenging cycling. The terrain on any route is the difference between the maximum and minimum heights on that route. For example if the route starts at a location at a height of 50 m and ascends a hill to 140 m, the difference is 90 m therefore the terrain is regarded as rolling terrain.

Roads give an indication of traffic volume. Unfortunately Dublin's suburbia continues to creep into the surrounding counties increasing traffic volumes, and making it less attractive for the cyclist, although provision is sometimes made for cyclists. However, all the routes stick to third-class roads as far as possible, and it's amazing the number of quiet roads there are still. Generally national primary and secondary roads are busy most of the time. Many regional roads are busy, particularly at commuting times, and third-class roads are sometimes used as rat runs. Third-class roads carry agricultural traffic which, although frustrating for the motorist, will not bother the cyclist too much, except perhaps for mud tracks left on wet days.

(OSI xx map): The appropriate 1:50,000 Ordnance Survey Map(s).

Attractions you are likely to meet along the way in terms of scenery, heritage, and flora and fauna.

BENEFITS OF CYCLING

There is nothing better than the freedom cycling offers on a good day along a quiet, country road. Hear the diverse sounds of the country-side and look in awe at its beauty. Singing birds, whispering breezes and rustling foliage are instruments of a natural concert. Stop when you feel like it, at the brow of a hill perhaps and take in the scene below, a carpet of green and lush land. Catch your breath and delight in the satisfaction that you have conquered the hill. Prepare to reap your reward, the exhilaration of freewheeling down the other side. As you continue on your way, allow your mind to dwell on the good things in life and formulate your plans to realise them. Relax and enjoy, you are in no rush to go anywhere.

The bicycle is a tremendously cost-effective and efficient means of transportation. As well as recreation, you can cycle for practical pur-poses such as going to work and to the shops. You can cycle on your own or with family and friends. There is no road tax, maintenance costs are very small and the bicycle is easy to park. It is much faster than walking and yet you can still fully sense the environment around you. The bicycle is environmentally friendly. There are no smoky exhausts and oil leaks, no noise except the soft whirr of the chain set. A bicycle takes up little space, will last you years, and give you hours of good clean fun.

Cycling is an excellent form of exercise, and benefits the cardio-vascular system. Generally leisure cycling is an aerobic work-out which is easier on the body than many other forms of exercise. It is one of the more comfortable forms of physical activity for those who are new to exercise, allowing most people to get fit easily without undue physical strain. It is beneficial to the lungs, which expand to gather as much oxygen into the body as possible, requiring the heart to beat faster and transport the oxygen around the body. A strong heart and sound lungs form the basis of general fitness. If you cycle regularly you will feel the difference. You should be able to climb that stairs without being short of breath, and cycling also helps to control weight.

Anxiety and stress too can be relieved, partly due to the physical activity itself and partly due to the pleasure and satisfaction of riding a bike. Cycling helps create a feeling of contentment and wellbeing and if you cycle in pleasant surroundings, well, all the better. The activity lends itself to the 'eureka' phenomenon, when that elusive problem is suddenly solved. It helps clear the fog of chaos, allows the mind to focus and puts things into perspective thereby allowing you to keep your sanity in a sometimes-chaotic world.

BICYCLE TYPES

You do not need a super-duper bicycle for the type of cycling this book promotes. The purpose is to get out there and enjoy cycling, as well as exploring the environment you pass through. Basically any machine will do once it's roadworthy, but the following gives a flavour of some common and suitable bikes.

Bicycles have developed over the centuries from the Fred-Flintstone, foot-paddling type to the sophisticated, foot-pedalling machines of today. Generally they can be classified into four popular types. The traditional road or racing bike has drop handlebars, light frame, narrow tyres and a gear system generally set high. It is designed for speed, but the narrow tyres do not perform well on poor road surfaces, and unless you are fit you may have to dismount on those steep gradients. Another form of road bike is the touring bike; it has more gears especially lower ones, and wider tyres. It is designed for long-distance touring over a variety of terrain and equipped for carrying a load. The mountain bike is a development of the BMX, which is a bike with a rugged frame and single gear designed for short dirt tracks. The mountain bike itself is rugged, with flat handlebars, lots of gears and broad, tractor-like tyres which are able to absorb poor road surfaces. They are good for off-road cycling. However, mountain bikes are inclined to be heavy and require more effort to push. A more recent addition is the hybrid bike. It is a mix of the others and has a light frame, tyres similar to a touring bike, and equipped with plenty of gears. Like the mountain bike it has flat handlebars. Generally flat handlebars offer only one riding position that may become uncomfortable when in the saddle a long time. Extensions are sometimes added for more flexibility. Drop handlebars are usually better for varying your riding position.

Bicycle costs range from hundreds to thousands of euro, and like everything else you pay for what you get. Generally the more you pay the lighter the machine and better the equipment.

COMFORT AND SAFETY

Cycling is made all the more enjoyable by following some basic suggestions to help keep you comfortable, moving and safe; much of it is common sense really.

Having a well-maintained bike that fits will help you get to the end of your journey comfortably and safely. Eating and drinking properly will prevent you from suffering the dreaded 'bonk' and from dehydrating, and wearing suitable clothing will increase your comfort. Taking account of the hazards on the road will reduce the risk of accident, and in the case of one wearing the right protection will lessen the risk of injury. Finally take account of the weather forecast when planning your cycle.

The right size bike

Having a bike that fits will get you off to a flying start and your dealer should advise you. However, here are some rules of thumb for choosing one:

(i) Stand astride the crossbar. Your crotch should clear the crossbar by 25–50 mm for a road bike and about 75 mm for a mountain bike.

(ii) Set the saddle so that with your heel on the pedal in the down position your leg is fully extended.

(iii) The height of the handlebars should be slightly lower than the height of the saddle and the width should be about the width of your shoulders.

If you are buying a bike make sure it fits you and don't take one just because of a special offer. It does not always work out in the long term.

Gearing

Sometimes cyclists rise to the challenge a hill offers and become dogged about cycling to the top by hook or by crook. But what's the point if when you get there you are in a lather of sweat, with lungs pumping like a bellows, trying to catch that elusive breath. The message here is, 'take it easy.' Stop to rest and enjoy the views, walk even — you will get to the top eventually. Of course having a good range of quality gears and using them correctly can mean getting to the top more efficiently and comfortably and, even better, without having to walk.

Modern bikes have plenty of gears, 21 being common. Gears are selected by shifting the chain between 6 or 7 sprockets on the back wheel and 2 or 3 chain-rings on the pedal cranks. Large chain rings combined with small sprockets deliver more speed but require more effort, whereas small chain rings and large sprockets take less effort at the expense of speed. The trick is to select a gear that allows you to pedal at a constant, comfortable rate, varying the gear to match the terrain or head wind. Avoid cycling in gears that are too high as this will trouble your knees. Too low a gear and you will be pedalling uncomfortably fast. Practise through the gears until you get a feel for the right one. An index gearshift is useful as each gear clicks positively into position, rather like synchronised gears in a car.

Maintenance

Bicycles are mechanical things and require maintenance to ensure that you reach your destination safely without incident, so keep your bike in good shape. It is also easier to fix your bike at home rather than at the roadside. Here are a few pre-cycle checks before you head off:

(i) Inspect your tyres for wear and air pressure.

(ii) Lift and spin each wheel — if they rub against the brake blocks there might be a broken or loose spoke to be repaired.

(iii) Inspect the brake pads and cables for wear and corrosion. Check that they operate correctly and adjust the cables if necessary.

(iv) Inspect the chain by back-pedalling, making sure it runs smoothly. Check gears are not slipping and gear cables are not worn or corroded.

(v) Make sure that all nuts and screws are tight.

If you are unsure about the condition of your bicycle bring it to a professional mechanic for a check.

It is better to cycle than walk, especially if you are miles from home, so carry some basic repair equipment:

(i) Pump,

(ii) Puncture repair kit,

(iii) Spare inner tube,

(iv) Basic tool kit including tyre levers.

Protection

Wearing the correct protection reduces the risk of injury if you are involved in an accident. Head protection is a must, so a good-quality helmet is well advised. Get one with a recognised safety standard such as those advised by the National Safety Council:

Snell-USA Standard

ANSI Z 904-USA Standard

BS6863-British Standard

AS2063-Australian Standard

If you happen to have a spill, padded mittens can help to reduce cuts and abrasions on the palms of your hands, and wearing sunglasses will not only shade your eyes from the sun, but may also help protect them from wind, dust and flying insects.

Motor vehicles account for most cycling fatalities and for serious injury. So make sure you are seen, particularly if you are cycling at night or in twilight. There are many aids to providing good visibility through a selection of lights and reflective wear available in good cycling stores. Even during the day you will be more visible if you wear bright colours.

As cycling is an all-year-round sport the seasons will determine the type of clothing you should wear to protect you from the weather. Remember that most of the routes in this book will have you out for several hours and more. However, the time includes plenty of rest periods, unless you decide otherwise. So you could get away with tracksuit bottoms in winter and shorts in summer. Jeans are not a good choice because of the restricted movement in them, and they take a long time to dry after getting wet. It is always advisable to carry rain-proof gear whilst cycling in any part of Ireland, and the east coast is no different. Stiff shoes help keep your feet from aching and padded mittens provide similar protection for your hands. In the winter you will need to wear extra layers. On a bike the temperature of your body varies: uphill you generate a lot of heat and sweat and downhill you get chilled by the apparent wind. Wear several thin layers rather than one thick layer as you can remove layers and replace them as appropriate. I got away with cycling all 40 tours wearing clothing as described above, and lived to write the book.

However, if you plan to spend long periods in the saddle and like to look the part then you could consider authentic cycle clothing. Cycling shorts and tights are seamless to prevent chafing, and provide padding for more comfort. The modern materials used are waterproof, windproof and breathable. And even if not waterproof they are quick to dry. The clothes are designed to be attractive and, as with all modern clothing, there are the labels if you are into them.

On the road

The routes in this book are mainly on third-class roads but sometimes you have to follow the busier regional and national roads. Whatever sort of road, you must cycle safely and be aware of other road users, both vehicular and pedestrian. Plan a move in advance by checking for traffic and signalling in plenty of time. Be aware that motorists may not always see you, so make allowances for them. Stay as close to the verge as possible taking road conditions into account. Potholes and broken verges are hazards; watch for them in time to avoid falling or swerving in front of an overtaking vehicle. Potholes in particular are difficult to spot when filled with water.

Mud, fallen leaves, and rain make the road slippery. Adjust your cycling speed to these conditions and be extra careful when rounding corners. Remember too that your brakes can be less effective in wet conditions. Frost and icy conditions should be avoided as should high winds, particularly on open roads, as gusts can knock you off balance.

When cycling in town be mindful of high kerbs as it is possible to catch the pedal on a down stroke, throwing you off. Time in the saddle will make you tired and can affect concentration which in turn increases risk of accident. Remember this book is all about leisure cycling, so rest often.

Consideration, too, must be given to animals. From time to time you will encounter dogs, cattle, sheep and horses amongst smaller creatures. Barking dogs can be a nuisance, and sometimes chase cyclists. Do not panic — stop, if necessary, to face the animal. An assertive voice can often put them off.

Of course most cycling passes without incident. However, in case of emergency dial 999 or 112 for the emergency services, which is a good reason to carry a mobile phone. But hopefully it will only be used to order a well-deserved dinner after the cycle.

Cycling in a group

When in a group, always cycle in a disciplined manner for your own safety and the safety of the others. Avoid cycling too close to the bicycle in front. Keep at least a bicycle length behind to give you time to brake and stop in an emergency. You may cycle two abreast on quiet roads but on the busier ones it may be more appropriate to ride in single file. If it becomes necessary to change from two abreast to single file then the outside rider normally falls behind the rider nearest the verge. Regular groups develop calls and hand signals that they use regularly. Everyone in the group should pass on a signal to make sure it travels the full length of the group, especially warnings from the rear, like overtaking vehicles. Remember too that only the front riders get a clear view of road defects, parked cars, route hazards etc. so it is important that they give clear indications in plenty of time to those behind.

Food and drink

The exertion of cycling will burn up carbohydrates quite quickly and more so in cold weather. If your tank runs out of carbohydrates, your energy levels fall and you get the dreaded 'bonk' — your legs suddenly feel heavy and your head light. The intake of suitable carbohydrate foods before and during exertion can improve performance, especially on long routes. So eat a good meal the night before a long cycle and eat regular, small portions during it. Remember too that your body can lose a lot of fluid through sweating and this can also affect your performance. It can happen before you feel thirsty so drink plenty and often, especially in hot weather. A drink should be carried for all but the shortest trips.

So, what might you eat and drink when on the road? Water and fat-free, sugar foods are good and the banana is the traditional cyclist's snack. Most of the routes pass through towns and villages where you can fill the tank while resting. And having a picnic at the side of the road on a good day can be very pleasant, and inexpensive.

Carrying provisions

Remember, too, you will need to carry food, extra clothing and emergency equipment, especially on the longer and more remote routes. You could carry these on a backpack but this can be uncomfortable — not just for the weight but also because of the cold feel of sweat on your back, made worse in warm weather. The alternative is to equip your bicycle with a pannier. These vary in size and fixing. Some are supported on frames fitted to the bike and others are fixed directly to the bicycle frame. Generally the latter are of the smaller variety and less expensive. Keep in mind, too, whether you want to support a map on the bike to save you having to take it out every time you want to refer to it — some handlebar panniers provide a waterproof map holder.

Weather

Probably the most popular topic of conversation around Dublin, as in Ireland as a whole, is the weather. Its changeability makes it a good source for casual chat, and more often than not instigates more weighty subjects. Generally Ireland has a mild, damp climate with rain occurring throughout the year. However, the east is in one of the driest parts of the country. Rainfall tends to be higher in winter than in summer. The annual number of days with more than 1 mm of rainfall is about 150 in the driest parts of the country. Average rainfall varies between 800 and 2,800 mm for the country as a whole.

The climate of Ireland is dominated by the effects of the Atlantic Ocean. The warm, Gulf-Stream current washes its shores and the prevailing winds are from the southwest. Consequently, Ireland does not suffer from the extreme temperature variations experienced by other countries at similar latitude. However, the temperatures on Ireland's east coast tend to be more extreme than the rest of the country. The daily mean maximum temperature for the east of the country is about

19°C in summer and the daily mean minimum temperature is about 2.5°C in winter.

Wind speeds tend to be higher in the west and lower in the east, and strong winds tend to be more frequent in winter. Mean annual wind speed for the country as a whole varies from 4 m/second in the east midlands to 7 m/second in the northwest. The routes in this book tend to go north, west and south from Dublin. With the prevailing winds from the southwest, this often means that the wind is in your face when starting out but on your back when returning, a welcome help-out for those tired legs.

It is always worth checking the weather before you start your journey so that you can dress appropriately or even decide whether to go or not. Bear in mind that it can be risky as well as unpleasant when cycling on mountain routes in inclement weather. On the flip side we can get hot, sunny days with temperatures well in excess of 20°C. On these days wear a good sunscreen as the cooling effect of a breeze can hide the sun's effect. You may not realise that you are sunburnt until too late. Remember, too, to drink more water in warm weather.

Ireland's regional weather forecasts can be found on the Met Eireann website *www.meteireann.ie* or in the media.

TRANSPORTING BICYCLES

Generally the routes in this book are within an hour's drive of Dublin City. Therefore you are going to have to transport your bicycle to the start of a route unless you live nearby or are willing to cycle to the start.

Iarnrod Eireann (01) 8366222 will carry bicycles when a train has a guard's van. Many of the trains around Dublin are DART/diesel commuters and do not have this facility, although you may manage a folding bike. Dublin Bus does not have a facility for carrying bicycles. Bus Eireann (01) 8366111 does, if you arrive in plenty of time. It depends on space in the luggage area, and there is a fixed charge. It's best to check with Iarnrod Eireann or Bus Eireann before going to a station.

If you own a motor vehicle or have access to one, this is probably the most flexible option to transport your bike. With an estate or hatchback you could probably carry one bike by removing its front wheel and putting down the car's rear seats. However, to carry up to three bicycles there is a selection of bicycle carriers that can easily be fixed to and removed from a vehicle. They range in price from about €70, at time of writing, upwards and you pay for what you get. Generally there are three types; one that is fixed to a ball hitch on a towbar, one fixed to a roof rack, and one fixed to a boot or hatch door. They all have their strengths and weaknesses. Bear in mind the number of bicycles you plan to carry before choosing. For the first type you will need a ball hitch on your car and if you do not have one, it is expensive to fit. You may find the second type awkward, having to lift bicycles on and off the roof. Check if the third type will block lights and number plate — if this is the case you may have to extend them. Shop around for the carrier that suits you best.

Maps and Finding Your Way

Generally around Dublin national and regional roads are well sign-posted, but not so well the third-class and lesser roads, and the cycling routes here adhere to these as much as possible. The maps in this book are rough guides to the routes described. They, along with the route descriptions, should be sufficient to find your way. Of course you can always ask a local if you do get lost. The route descriptions provide distances between key points along a route, and so it is useful to carry an instrument for measuring trip distance. This feature, amongst others, is usually incorporated in bicycle computers which are relatively inexpensive now, and can be mounted on the handlebar for viewing.

I would recommend the Ordnance Survey (OSI) Discovery Series of maps. They are ideal for this sort of cycle exploring. Generally one or two maps will cover each of the routes. The series numbers are given in the summary at the beginning of each route so that you can buy what you need. Nine OSI maps cover all the routes: 36, 42, 43, 49, 50, 55, 56, 61, 62, but generally one or two will cover each. The scale is 1:50,000 and they show 10-m contours, a useful indication of hill gradients. They also include locations of castles, martello towers, holy wells and more. The maps are available at major bookstores or directly from Ordnance Survey Ireland.

Generally a bigger scale map is more appropriate for driving to route starts. An OSI 1:250,000 map for the East of Ireland is more than satisfactory, or a National 1:400,000 will also do.

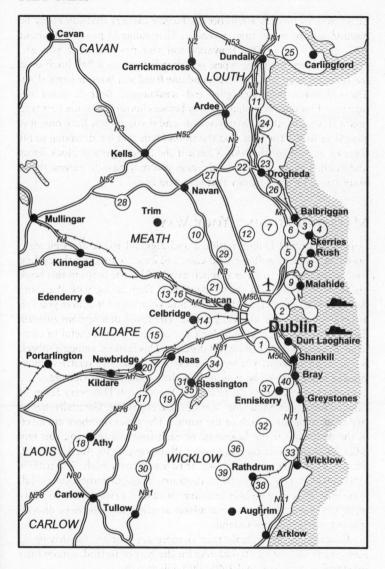

1. Fairy Castle Pub Crawl (Dublin)

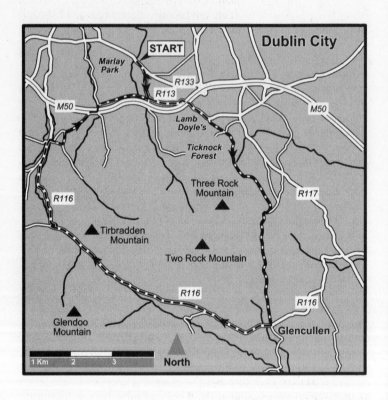

1. Fairy Castle Pub Crawl (Dublin)

Distance (km)	20
Cycling time (hours)	$2^1/_2$
Terrain	Mountainous
Roads (osi 50 map)	Two-thirds on regional, the remaining on third-class. Busy stretch around Marlay Park. Route can be busy on weekends and holidays
Attractions	Mountains, Woodland, a little Heritage, Old pubs

Nature is truly magnificent in the mountains, and people view the raw environment in awe. This challenging cycle explores the mountains that dominate South County Dublin and also passes a number of landmark pubs. Low gears will be well exercised on this one, as you crawl up the hills. Even a little walking may suit you on the steeper climbs. However, the hard work will be rewarded with beautiful views and, remember, what goes up must come down, so you can also enjoy freewheeling downhill. I chose the 214-acre Marlay Park to start as there is abundant parking here. The route first goes east of the mountains on the coast side where there are fine views over Dublin Bay and City, whereas on the west side, the route passes between several mountains patched with coniferous forests. These mountains were created over 10,000 years ago during the Ice Age, a very turbulent time indeed. But the result is wonderful and they are there for us to enjoy today.

For many the M50 is the most convenient option to get to the start of this route. Drive south and leave at exit 13, for Dundrum/Sandyford. At the roundabout take a left towards Rathfarnham. Marlay Park is about 2 km away on your left and there is a signpost before the entrance. You can park your car here.

From Marlay Park turn right — there is a cycle track across the road. Cycle to the junction at the R113 and turn right again, following the sign toward Stepaside. Soon you will face Taylors Three Rock thatched pub. The lands of the Taylor family once formed a border with the Pale, an area surrounding Dublin. The Pale marked the jurisdiction of English rule in Ireland during the Middle Ages. Basically it was a fortified trench outside of which you were 'beyond the Pale'.

3

1. Fairy Castle Pub Crawl (Dublin)

And beyond the Pale, the Irish clans ruled with their Norman allies who had gone native. They were fond of harassing the English from time to time but never managed to drive them out.

Turn left at the traffic lights at Taylors and follow the road to cross a bridge over the M50. Be careful here because on breezy days the winds funnel across the bridge and could knock you off balance. Take the second right at Lamb Doyle's Pub onto a third-class road, about 3 km from Marlay Park. When you look at this modern establishment now it's hard to believe it was once a simple bar and grocery, but progress brings prosperity. From here the going gets hard, as the climb is steep. On your right you will see Three Rock Mountain, recognisable by the telecommunication masts rather than the rocky juts that gave it its name. On the left is Dublin Bay and City and you could stop here and spend time identifying the City landmarks. On the day I was there I saw the HSS high-speed ferry sail toward Dun Laoghaire, having traversed the Irish Sea from Holyhead. I understand it has to slow down well outside port to prevent its wash from causing waves in the harbour. I can just imagine all those yachts bobbing about, worrying their moorings.

Eventually you will reach the Blue Lite Pub in Barnacullia, a place to rest and enjoy marvellous views, after the hard climb. Then continue to a T-junction and take a right to Glencullen, about 3 km from here. Evidence of giant deer was found in Ballybetagh Bog near Glencullen. These massive Irish elk were 2 m high at the shoulder and had antlers up to 4 m. Imagine one grazing as you pass by and he slowly looking up. What would he have made of you and your bicycle? Anyway, these ancient creatures are said to be older than the surrounding mountains. They were victims of the Ice Age which formed these mountains — amazing!

You will arrive at Johnnie Fox's Pub in Glencullen. Established in 1798, this pub is said to be the highest in Ireland, which begs the question, would alcohol go quicker to your head here? Glencullen itself is nestled in a beautiful, natural setting of rugged mountains and deep valleys. In the cemetery are the remains of an old church. At Johnnie Fox's Pub, turn right onto the R116. There is a steady climb out of Glencullen with Two Rock Mountain on your right and the cairn, Fairy Castle, perched on top. On the left you should see Glendoo Mountain. About 2 km from Glencullen you will come across signs for

1. Fairy Castle Pub Crawl (Dublin)

the famous Wicklow Way. This 130-km scenic walk begins at Marlay Park and travels across South Dublin and Wicklow to finish in Clonegal, County Carlow. Near the signs I saw a grey squirrel bounding across the ground between trees. I understand they can leap 6 m and I tried to calculate how long one would take to climb to the Fairy Castle Cairn at 536 m. As you descend you will pass Tibradden pine forest on your right, whose trees skirt Tibradden Mountain. Just past is a T-junction; go right. Continue descending, with the City in view, to a junction where you turn right, off the R116 onto the R113, for Leopardstown/Dundrum and an almost immediate left onto the Tibradden Road (R113). Follow the road to a roundabout at the M50 motorway. Turn left here and go under the motorway, and then immediate right. Follow the wall around Marlay Park, taking two lefts, back to the main entrance to pick up your car. Look for the cycle track at the second left.

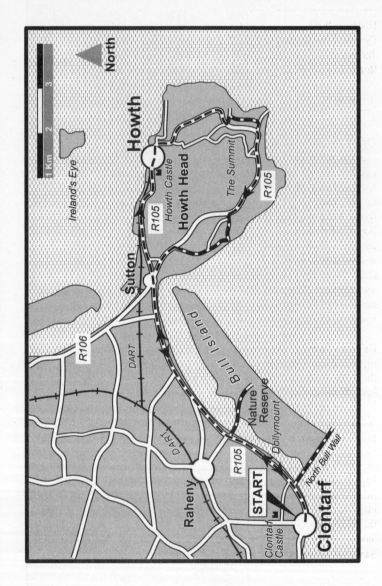

2. Brian Boru Circuit (Dublin, Fingal)

Distance (km)	44
Cycling time (hours)	5
Terrain	Hilly (in part)
Roads (OSI 50 map)	Three-quarters on cycle track, remainder on a mix of regional and third-class
Attractions	Coast, Park, Wildlife sanctuary, Heritage

Of all the routes in this book this is the nearest to Dublin City, yet the coast is never far from sight and there are great opportunities to see wildlife. A cycle track is available most of the way, much of which is off-road and away from the traffic. The terrain is quite flat except for a climb to the Summit at Howth. The route begins at Clontarf near the Alfie Byrne Road and hugs the coast. There are great views across busy Dublin Bay to the peninsula of Howth. It passes St Anne's Park, the second largest in Dublin, before detouring onto Bull Island. This protected area is abundant with wildlife. The route continues to Sutton where the coast is left behind for a while. From Howth Harbour, Ireland's Eye can be seen through the masts of working and pleasure boats. Then climb to the summit of Howth for the magnificent views over Dublin Bay. After, the route descends to Sutton and back to your waiting car.

Drive to Fairview from the City centre. Pass by Fairview Park on the right and under the arched, railway bridge. The next junction is with the Alfie Byrne Road. Watch for the car park on the right just past here. If the car park is full, there are others further on.

Once on your bike, use the off-road cycling track to continue. The architecture along the coast road changes from late 18th-century to the present day, and Dublin Bay is in full view from the peninsula of Howth to the River Liffey. Going back a thousand years or so, imagine the fear in the Irish camp when the masts of the Viking longships appeared across this wide horizon, their sails bulging with menace, and filled with crews ravenous for the spoils of Ireland. This is what greeted High King Brian Boru as he prepared to make his final stand against the Norsemen. A man of 70 years, he was a seasoned campaigner having taken on the ancient Scandinavians several times before. The Battle of Clontarf in 1014 was to be a final clash with his old enemy.

7

2. Brian Boru Circuit (Dublin, Fingal)

You will soon pass 2 churches on the left, St Anthony's and Clontarf Methodist, before coming to Castle Avenue, 4th left after the churches. There is a sign for Clontarf Castle. You can dismount and cross the road using the pedestrian lights. Halfway up Castle Avenue, in the wall on the right-hand side, is Brian Boroimh's well. Here a plaque was erected in 1850 that looks like a cast-iron door in the wall, and brightly coloured it is too. The well is associated with Brian Boru and the famous Battle of Clontarf. The actual battle began in the morning with each army facing each other and roaring insults. Individual scores were first settled, cheered on by their own side. Eventually the main groups clashed. Brian Boru was too old to take an active part. He remained behind the Irish lines while his eldest son Murchad led the Irish in the field. The bloody battle raged for most of the day with heavy losses on both sides. Finally the Irish got the upper hand and routed the Norsemen. They fled to their ships but the tide had come in and they either drowned or were slaughtered along the shoreline. In the meantime, while Brian was praying in his tent, some of his fleeing enemy managed to kill him and his bodyguards. Although the Irish won this great battle the cost was high for both sides. The death of Brian Boru and his son led to a destructive power struggle amongst the chieftains, and it set in motion the decline of Norse power.

Continue up Castle Avenue to Clontarf Castle, now a fine hotel. Originally an Anglo-Norman stronghold, it eventually fell to the Vernon family who were associated with it for several centuries. Around 1827 the original castle was deemed unsafe, and the one you see was built in a Tudor revival style. Return to the cycle track on the coast road, and continue past the Church of John the Baptist and Clontarf village, about 1.5 km from the start. Note the Moai sculpture on the grass. This is a replica of an Easter Island head or *Moai*. It was sculptured using volcanic stone from the island. Soon after is the Bull Wall, a popular walk that leads to North Bull Island. Access is over a wooden bridge. You should dismount as cycling is prohibited across the bridge. The main building on the island is the clubhouse for the prestigious Royal Dublin Golf Club, founded in 1885. There is also a second golf club, St Anne's. The Bull Wall itself was recommended in 1800 by Captain William Bligh of 'Mutiny on the Bounty' fame. His proposal was to build a north wall parallel with the existing South

Wall to reduce sand silting the entrance to the port of Dublin. Bligh's plan was modified so that the two walls would be at an angle so as to contain more water. This improved the sand-scouring effect of the ebb tide. At the far end of the Bull Wall is a tall structure on top of which is a statue called Our Lady of the Port of Dublin. Further out past the breakwater is the North Bull Lighthouse, painted green for starboard navigation. Opposite on the South Wall is Poolbeg Lighthouse, painted red for port navigation, and nearby are the tall, red-striped stacks of ESB's Poolbeg Power Station.

Return to the cycle track, which at this stage ends for about 1.5 km. The next feature is St Anne's Park, about 1 km from the Bull Wall. The park, famous for its rose garden, covers 266 acres of landscaped grounds. It was the former home of the Guinness family of brewing fame. The grounds were planted *c.* 1880 using evergreen holm-oak and pine to provide shelter from the sea winds. Near the far end of the park, I saw a chipmunk foraging alongside a grey squirrel. Chipmunks are not native to Ireland, and so this one may have escaped or was released from captivity. They are found in Siberia and North America — this one looked to be of the Siberian variety.

The cycle track reappears near the end of St Anne's Park. A little further is another road to North Bull Island. This will take you to the Nature Reserve and Interpretative Centre. The Island has grown substantially since Captain Bligh's day. Accumulated sand forms new dunes that are strengthened by marram grass. Around the island, the mudflats, sandflats and salt marshes have become important breeding grounds for a wide array of birds. Species such as the brent-goose, redshank and knot come here in internationally important numbers. Return to the cycle track and continue. After about 3 km you will pass Kilbarrack Graveyard in which are the remains of a 16th-century church, and another 1.5 km will take you to busy Sutton Cross. Continue straight through the traffic lights for about 2 km to Howth Castle. The Norman knight Sir Almeric Tristram was granted the manor of Howth by Henry II for services given in defeating the Norsemen on St Lawrence's Day. Sir Almeric adopted the saint's name and the St Lawrence family have been associated with Howth ever since. Sir Almeric's sword is preserved in Howth Castle, the family residence. The present castle was built in 1564 and located on the site of an earlier one. Queen Grace O'Malley from Mayo, also known as

2. Brian Boru Circuit (Dublin, Fingal)

Grainuaile, returned through Howth after visiting Queen Elizabeth I of England. She found the gates of the castle closed to her at mealtime. Seeing red, she kidnapped the young heir to Lord Howth and brought him to her castle in Mayo. She held him hostage until she got a written promise from Lord Howth that the gates would never be closed to her again.

Return to the main road and continue to Howth, dominated by its harbour 1 km away, and to where the cycle track ends. Howth is rich in legend and history. But more recently, it was the scene of gun-running in 1914. Nine hundred rifles were smuggled into the country on the yacht *Asgard*, owned by Erskine Childers. These were delivered to Irish Volunteers led by Cathal Brugha and destined for use in the failed uprising in 1916. The harbour was built between 1807 and 1814. On the nearer west pier are the embedded and dainty footprints of King George IV who visited in 1821. There are plenty of fish shops along the pier if you fancy cooking later.

At the east pier car park turn right and at the nearby Abbey Tavern are steps that will take you to St Mary's Abbey, founded *c*. 14th century. There are fine views of the harbour and Ireland's Eye from here. Return to the road and continue. Keep left of the church as you begin a steep ascent. At the Summit Inn turn left for the Summit. From the car park here there are fabulous views across Dublin Bay. Return to take the first left, before the main road you turned off. The road descends through a very exclusive area, with fine houses secured behind ornate gates. At a stop sign, turn left. From here the views over the bay are magnificent. Take a left at the sign for Sutton Strand. The descent is very steep and will exercise your brakes. At the bottom of the hill at a stop sign turn right. Continue on, turning left onto the main road (R105) towards Sutton Cross, about 4 km away, and passing St Fintan's Church on the right. At Sutton Cross turn left onto the cycling lane, and continue straight back to your car, about 10 km away.

3. Fingal Circuit (Fingal, Meath)

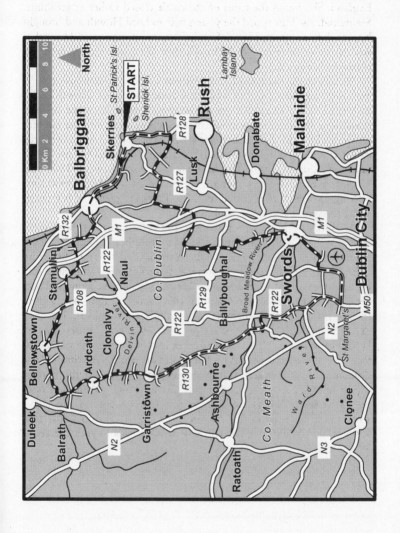

3. Fingal Circuit (Fingal, Meath)

Distance (km)	91
Cycling time (hours)	7
Terrain	Part hilly
Roads (osi 43, 50 maps)	Three-quarters on third-class, remainder on regional
Attractions	Coast, Rolling countryside, Airport, some Heritage

This long cycle presents an opportunity to traverse much of Ancient Fingal and a little of Royal Meath too. You will need to keep exploration to a minimum though to complete the route in one day. Although it goes over ground covered on other routes there are also new places to visit, such as Bellewstown in Meath and St Margaret's in Fingal. The terrain is quite easy going but for hills at Bellewstown, Garristown and the Man O' War. At first the route has a coastal flavour running from Skerries to Balbriggan before moving inland through Stamullin to the old horseracing venue at Bellewstown. It then turns to Ardcath and Garristown before stretching to St Margaret's and Dublin Airport. For those interested in plane-spotting this is the place. Heading north past Swords, the route follows quiet, third-class roads to the Man O' War situated on the original main road to the North. It then turns towards the coast and back to Skerries via Loughshinny.

Take the M1 from the City past the airport, and then take the exit for Skerries. Follow the signs, turning right onto the R127 at Blake's Cross and driving through Lusk. To enter Skerries you must drive through a railway tunnel. Turn left at the roundabout here and continue for 1 km to the obelisk known locally as 'the monument'. Go left and then right towards the harbour. Keep right on the Y-junction to bring you onto the South Strand. There is some free parking along the beach here. (A parking alternative is Skerries Mills, but mind the closing times.) Skerries is about 30 km from the City.

Cycle back the way you drove in as far as the traffic lights at the junction with the Balbriggan Road. Turn right here at the sign for Balbriggan. On leaving Skerries the coast and Balbriggan, about 7 km away, come into view. On a clear day you should see as far as the Mourne Mountains. This is a very scenic cycle although the road can be busy. About 3 km from Balbriggan, you will pass under the pedestrian bridge leading to Ardgillan Castle. The Dublin-to-Belfast railway line is to your left. When opened on 15 March 1844, the line went as far as Drogheda. A puffing steam locomotive, 'The Nora Creina', hauled 7 carriages with 565 passengers on board from Dublin to Drogheda in 100 minutes. Today it takes about half that time on board a diesel commuter.

On approaching Balbriggan turn left over the railway bridge. Soon after take the fork to the right, following the sign for Drogheda. Continue to a T-junction, just past Balbriggan's Carnegie Library on the right. This impressive building with its unusual conical clock tower was built in 1905. Turn right at the junction onto the R132 (old N1) in the direction of Drogheda. Soon after turn left at traffic lights onto the R122, following a sign for the Naul. After 2 km, turn right onto a third-class road at the sign for Balscaddan. This road rises before falling to a left turn surrounded by a community of houses, 2 km from the R122. This will take you through Balscaddan. The area was the birthplace of St Benignus. When he was very young St Patrick met his father Sesegne. When St Patrick left, Benignus followed and Patrick allowed him on his mission, serving as a psalm singer. Eventually Benignus became a priest and succeeded Patrick as Bishop of Armagh.

Pass through Balscaddan and cross the motorway, eventually coming to a stop sign at a T-junction, about 1.5 km from the village. The day I was here a sign to the left indicated that the Naul was 75 km. I could only presume that some creative character had added an authentic looking 7 in front of the 5. Anyway you will turn right towards Stamullin, about 1 km, rather than left. Once in Stamullin turn left to a branch junction 0.5 km away. Take the middle road in the direction of Bellewstown, about 6 km. There is a steady climb to a T-junction where you turn right onto the R108. Here the road signs were hidden behind a tree. After a few hundred metres veer left off the R108, still following the signs for Bellewstown. Cycle straight across the next crossroads and the road then ascends into Bellewstown to a height of around 140 m. On the outskirts, at a yield sign, turn right to the crossroads around the village centre. On the right of the crossroads is the racecourse. The first horseracing here was recorded in 1726. But what put Bellewstown on the racing map was George Tandy, a former Mayor of Drogheda and a brother of the more famous Napper Tandy. He persuaded King George III to sponsor a race at Bellewstown in 1780. The race, valued at £100, was called His Majesty's Plate. The English monarchs continued to sponsor a race at Bellewstown until 1980, when Queen Elizabeth II decided to call a halt.

Turn left at the crossroads in Bellewstown towards Ardcath about 7 km away, passing the Cosy Bar and the church. After 4 km you come to a stop sign at a T-junction, then turn left following the sign for Ardcath, 3 km. After 1 km you come to another stop sign at a crossroads, turn left. Keep right on the Y-junction which follows soon after. There is a climb into Ardcath, and after passing through the village the road tumbles towards Garristown, 4 km away. Surprisingly for the area there is a very straight section of road for a couple of kilometres. About 1 km from Garristown the road rises from about 80 m to 140 m just south of the village. It is hard to believe that this tranquil place was once the scene of a great ancient battle. The Battle of Gabhra came about when Cairbre, son of Cormac Mac Airt, became High King of Ireland. He planned to break the Fianna as he feared their threat to his own position; so he raised a great army to face them. Although the Fianna were well outnumbered, casualties were high on both sides and included the leader of the Fianna, Fionn Mac Cumhaill. The Fianna were finally beaten with only a small number surviving the fierceness of battle. Thereafter their power was broken in Ireland forever.

Cycle through Garristown and on the southern outskirts the road begins to descend. Continue cycling on the R130 for about 9 km to the junction with the R125. Go straight across following the sign for Finglas, continuing on the R130. After 1 km take a left for 1 km to the R122, and then turn right onto it. Continue on this road to St Margaret's, about 6 km away. On the way you will pass Corrstown Golf Club and St Margaret's Golf and Country Club before entering the village. You will then come to a stop sign, turn right. Detour at the next right before the roundabout to see Dunsoghly Castle situated on private lands. The castle, built around 1450 by Sir Rowland Plunkett, was continuously occupied by his descendants until around the 1870s. Unusually the roof has survived and was used as a model for restoration work at Bunratty Castle in County Clare and Rothe House in Kilkenny. There are also the ruins of a small chapel. The year 1573 is

14

3. Fingal Circuit (Fingal, Meath)

over the door, along with the Instruments of the Passion and the initials of John Plunkett and his wife Genet Sarsfield. I wonder what Sir Rowland himself would have thought of the airplanes now screaming over his property every 3 minutes or so.

Return to the main road and turn right towards the roundabout. At the roundabout turn left and follow the road around the airport. If you are interested you could rest for a while and watch the various aircraft take off and land. Continue past the Boot Inn on the right, and soon after on the left is a rather unkempt commemoration to the Forrest Inn. Like the Boot Inn it was a tavern that served the old Dublin-to-Drogheda coach road. Soon after you will come to a stop sign, turn right to a roundabout. Cycle straight across the roundabout, following the sign for Swords. Pass the radar station on the left and take the next left turn, following the sign for Forrest Little. Cycle passed Forrest Little Golf Club and on into Swords, the administrative capital of Fingal. At the traffic lights by the Lord Mayor's Pub turn left, and left again almost immediately. Pass by St Columba's Church on the left to the junction with the R125. Turn left and immediately after, at the traffic lights, turn right. Follow the road to a stop sign and turn left; to the right is a bridge over the Ward River. Cycle on through the traffic lights to the outskirts of Swords, and pass over the Broad Meadow River leaving Swords behind now.

About 3 km from Swords is the Dublin Butterfly House & Insect World. This tropical world presents an opportunity to view beautiful and rare butterflies as well as insects and other creatures in natural habitats. There is an entry fee and opening times are seasonal. Continue on for about 2 km to a crossroads with a cul-de-sac facing you, turn right here. After 1 km you will come to a junction with the R129. Cycle straight across. Cycle on for about 3 km to a T-junction and turn right. After another 2 km you will pass over the M1 motorway, and soon after arrive at a junction with the N1 at Ballough. There is a pub facing you. Turn left and immediate right following the signpost for the Man O' War. After 3 km of gradual ascent you will come to the Man O' War Pub on the left, established in 1595. There was once a turnpike or tollbooth here when this was the main Drogheda road. Things haven't changed much since except perhaps that bridges are tolled now.

At the pub turn right and after 2 km you will come to the junction with the R127. Turn left following the sign for Skerries and soon after,

3. Fingal Circuit (Fingal, Meath)

right following the sign for Baldungan Castle. Cycle on to Loughshinny Cross, about 4 km away, passing the castle ruins on the right. At Loughshinny Cross turn left for Skerries, about 5 km. There are nice views along the way. In Skerries you can replenish in many of the town's facilities, including the interesting Skerries Mills.

4. Fair Fingal (Fingal)

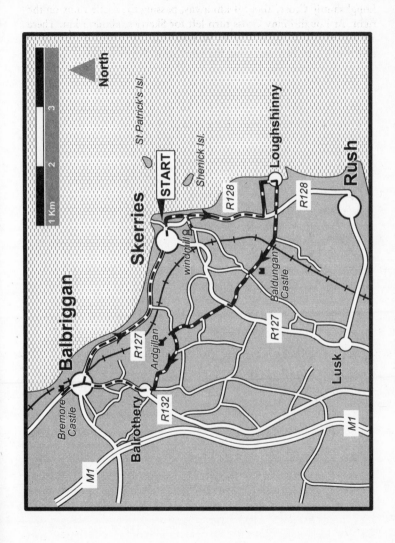

Distance (km)	30
Cycling time (hours)	$2^1/2$
Terrain	Mainly rolling
Roads (OSI 43 map)	Half third-class and half regional
Attractions	Coast, Gardens, Windmills, Heritage

This is a lovely cycle offering breathtaking views of the coast and rolling countryside of north Fingal. The start is a little hilly but the going gets easier. The road between Balbriggan and Skerries can be busy, though well worth the effort as the views are magnificent.

The route begins in Skerries, a town unique for its offshore islands and windmills. It rises toward the quaint village and harbour at Loughshinny where abundant and noisy oystercatchers can often be seen scuttling across the beach. Veering from the coast, the route then passes Baldungan Castle and Ardgillan Demesne before descending to Balrothery (the town of the knights). The busy town of Balbriggan is the next stop with its quaint harbour overlooked by the arched viaduct carrying the Dublin–Belfast railway line. The final section back to Skerries hugs the coast and there are beautiful views of Skerries, its islands and Rockabill Lighthouse. On summer weekends you can enjoy the colourful sails of the racing fleets.

Take the M1 from the City past the airport, and then take the exit for Skerries. Follow the signs, turning right onto the R127 at Blake's Cross and driving through Lusk. To enter Skerries you must drive through a railway tunnel. Turn left at the roundabout here and continue for 1 km to the obelisk known locally as 'the monument'. Go left and then right towards the harbour. Keep right on the Y-junction to bring you onto the South Strand. There is some free parking along the beach here. (A parking alternative is Skerries Mills, but mind the closing times.) Skerries is about 30 km from the City.

Cycle on along the South Strand and note the lighthouse and three islands offshore. Seven kilometres off the coast are two massive rocks; the large one is called the *rock* and the small one the *bill*. On top of the *rock* stands Rockabill Lighthouse. The rocks are a bird sanctuary, and support the largest colony of roseate terns in Europe. From left to right

4. Fair Fingal (Fingal)

the islands are Colt, St Patrick's and Shenick. Legend has it that St Patrick lived on St Patrick's Island. He owned a goat that supplied first-rate milk. During one of his visits to the mainland, locals stole his goat and ate it. The saint returned and was most upset. When challenged, the locals denied any knowledge of the missing goat. Their persistent denials turned to bleating, sounding like the goat they had eaten. When finally they admitted the truth their voices returned. The people of Skerries still carry the legacy. They are afflicted with the name 'Skerries Goat'. The window frame in the ruins on St Patrick's Island contains the outline of St Patrick, surely a sign that he was there?

The road veers away from the South Strand to a T-junction with the R128. Turn left here and immediate right to see Skerries Mills. Two windmills and a water mill, with millpond and millraces, have been restored to working order. They depict an efficient and clean use of water and wind power from the 17th, 18th and 19th centuries. The site also includes a coffee shop and a craft shop, and is open daily. Return to the main road (R128) and continue on towards Rush. About 3 km from Skerries the road rises quite sharply and there are pleasant views behind. Once over the hill you can freewheel to the speed restriction at Loughshinny. Turn left just past the speed restriction. Note the three standing stones in the small park here. These introduce local walks that take in historic sites and events. Follow the minor road to a T-junction where a small thatched cottage faces you. Detour left to bring you to the quaint harbour of Loughshinny. There is a martello tower marking the Drumanagh headland facing the harbour. This headland contains the remains of the largest promontory fort in Ireland. The 40-acre site is protected on three sides by cliffs and on the landside by ramparts stretching the width of the site. The site has never been fully excavated but it is thought to date from the Late Bronze/Early Iron Age. Roman coins were found on the headland, and this leads some to believe that Romans landed here, or at the very least locals traded with them in Britain.

Return to the thatched cottage and cycle past it. The road rises for 2 km eventually coming to a crossroads. Cycle straight across in the direction of Lusk. Baldungan Castle is about 2 km away, and at 70 m the site is one of the highest points in the area. The view southerly towards Howth and Lambay Island is particularly stunning. It is said that you can see 7 counties from here (try to figure out what they are). The remains at Baldungan consist of a fortified church originally dedicated to the Virgin Mother. Baldungan Castle itself was located just northwest of the church and is now completely gone. It was built shortly after the Anglo-Norman invasion by the Knights Templar, a monastic military order formed at the end of the First Crusade to the Holy Land. They were defeated around 1313 and the castle changed hands several times. Extended over the centuries, it became formidable by the mid-17th, and consisted of a square with four towers of equal height, similar to the remains of the church tower. During the Cromwellian War it was blown up. The castle was never repaired and over the intervening years gradually disappeared.

Continue for another 1 km to the junction with the R127. Turn right followed by a left nearby at the sign for Ardgillan Demesne. Cycle 1.5 km to a T-junction and turn left following the sign that will take you to Ardgillan. The grounds and views from Ardgillan Demesne are magnificent. There are a number of attractions: you can take a historic tour of the castle (really a castellated mansion), furnished in Victorian style; you can amble through the beautiful gardens; or relax at the coffee shop. There is also a rose garden, a walled herb garden and a Victorian conservatory. The Down Survey Exhibition (a series of survey maps from 1654) is also open to the public. The castle and tea-rooms are open from Tuesday to Sunday, and on public holidays.

On leaving Ardgillan Demesne turn right towards Balrothery, 3 km away. At the next T-junction turn right and descend into Balrothery. There is a fine 180°-view ahead from the coast inland. On entering Balrothery turn right at the small roundabout. Although a sleepy village, Balrothery was once an important place. It is known as the Town of the Knights. In 1200, King Henry II entrusted the Norman knight, Geoffrey de Constantyn, with the manor of Balrothery. Note the local ruins on your left, near the pub, part of which date back to this time.

Take the left turn just before the pub and follow the road round to the R132 (old N1). Turn right in the direction of Balbriggan. One of Ireland's greatest cyclists, 'The Balbriggan Flyer', came from the town — Harry Reynolds won the world amateur mile championship in Copenhagen in 1896. Shortly afterwards he turned professional and went on a world tour. He retired in 1901, but made a comeback in

1906 and won the National Cycling Union professional championship that year. He continued to compete for a number of years and was known for his endurance and grit. As you enter Balbriggan the imposing church of St Peter and Paul is beyond the roundabout. Cross the roundabout and continue for about 1 km through the town and past the Garda barracks. Watch for Bremore Castle on your right, the entrance is easily missed. This medieval structure has few parallels in Ireland, making it of great interest to architectural historians. Originally owned by the Barnewalls, it is now being restored through FAS and Fingal County Council.

Return to the centre of town and just past the sign for Skerries turn left at a Chinese restaurant. This will bring you to the harbour, seen through the arches of the viaduct carrying the Dublin–Belfast railway line. The lighthouse at the end of the pier was built in 1769. Go right at the Y-junction under one of the arches to take you back to Skerries. The railway line will be on your right. As you leave the built-up areas, the sea appears to your left. The views towards Skerries are delightful. After 3 km you pass under the 'Ladies Stairs'. This pedestrian bridge got its name from the ladies of Ardgillan who used it to gain access to the sea for bathing. Soon after is Barnageeragh, whose secluded beach is surrounded by tall cliffs. The road veers left here, and another 3 km will take you into Skerries. At the traffic lights turn left and cycle back to 'the monument', and then to your car. If you fancy coffee, the coffee shop at Skerries Mills is nice.

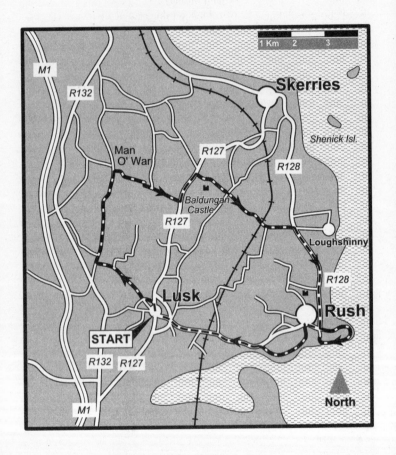

5. Lambay Views (Fingal)

Distance (km)	25
Cycling time (hours)	$2^1/2$
Terrain	Verging on hilly
Roads (OSI 43 map)	Two-thirds on third-class, the remainder on regional
Attractions	Coastal views, Bird-watching, some Heritage

This cycle verges on the hilly, but is rewarded with some great views along the south Fingal coast, and in particular Lambay Island where the sinking of the Tayleur *took place in the 19th century, a terrible tragedy of the time. But firstly, the route begins at Lusk, which they say was a village when Dublin was a swamp. It then ascends to the Man O' War where one of the oldest pubs in Ireland is located, and the views are quite spectacular to boot. Afterwards descend towards Loughshinny, cycling on some tranquil back-roads along the way. Nearby Loughshinny is the grave of a famous Robin-Hood-type character, Jack the Bachelor. Continue into Rush and to its quaint harbour, before cycling to its second harbour at Rogerstown. The estuary here presents a myriad of birds for the keen birdwatcher. Finally the route finishes back in ancient Lusk.*

Take the M1 from the City and after passing the airport, exit to Skerries. Follow the signs to Skerries and you will arrive at Lusk first, about 22 km from the City. You should find parking around the village centre.

The old church and round tower dominate the village. St Macullin, an early Christian convert, founded a church at Lusk *c.* 450 AD. Later, Norsemen burned the church and village *c.* 854 AD. The round tower may have been built around this time to protect the monks and treasures from the Norsemen. It dominates the skyline, but the current pace of local building development may change this. The site comprises the round tower, a medieval belfry, and a 19th-century church, all of which form a unit built over a thousand years. The belfry contains a magnificent 16th-century effigy tomb of Sir Christopher Barnewall and his wife Dame Marion. He died in 1575.

Cycle up Main Street towards Skerries and beyond the Top Shop Pub turn left at the pedestrian traffic lights. Soon after, you pass the more modern St Macullin's Church and then leave Lusk behind. As you cycle, the Dublin Mountains steal into view on the left, if the day is clear. There is a T-junction about 3 km from Lusk, turn right here in the direction of Balrothery. From here the road ascends all the way to the Man O' War Pub, about 3 km away. This establishment goes back to 1595 and served the great North Road. It was regarded at the time as 'one of the most commodious and best inns in this kingdom'. Wolfe Tone had an Irish breakfast there in July 1792. A little further on is the Man O' War Coach House, now being redeveloped.

Turn right at the pub, and ascend a bit more. The height here is about 100 m above sea level. Stop to admire the view before the road descends. To the south are the Dublin Mountains, southeast is the Howth Peninsula with Ireland's Eye at its edge, and in an easterly direction is Lambay Island. Lambay Island will dominate many of the views from here on.

Descend the hill and after 2.5 km you will come to a junction with the R127, turn left in the direction of Skerries. Shortly after, about 1 km, turn right and cycle to Baldungan Castle a little over 1 km away on the right. All that remains of this great castle is a ruined church. Founded by the Norman monastic military, Order of the Knights Templar, it was blown up during the Cromwellian War. The castle was never repaired and over the intervening years gradually disappeared, but the views are magnificent.

Continue to Loughshinny Cross, and at the stop sign turn right (R128) in the direction of Rush, about 3 km away. About 0.5 km on the left is Lizzy's Cottage, a fine example of an 18th-century thatched farmhouse. It has been restored and is privately owned. After another 0.5 km, on the right at the sign for St Catherine's Estate, is Kenure cemetery containing the grave of Jack the Bachelor, a famous smuggler. The coastal area around Rush was renowned for smuggling during the late 18th century. The smuggling trade became lucrative after the British Government imposed excise duties on a number of goods including brandy, rum and tea, which were known as 'run goods'. Jack Connors, known as Jack the Bachelor, found his niche in smuggling. But he was also a 'Robin Hood' character and many stories circulated of his generosity to the poor. Along with Captain Fields of Rush, he sailed 'run goods' into the area for two decades, evading capture by customs. He was buried at the young age of 36 in the old graveyard here and his funeral attracted a huge gathering of appreciative locals.

5. Lambay Views (Fingal)

Detour into St Catherine's to see all that remains of the great Kenure House. Only the portico stands, a peculiarity in a modern housing estate. Built in the 1800s by the Palmers, it remained with the family until 1963. Rising maintenance costs forced the family to sell it to the Land Commission. The mansion was demolished in 1978 as no one could be found to restore it. The movie '10 Little Indians' was made here in 1965. Directed by George Pollock, it tells Agatha Christie's tale of 10 people invited to an isolated place, only to find that an unseen person is killing them one by one.

Return to the R128 and continue. The town of Rush now comes into view. Approaching the town, to your left is the fine little Kenure Church built in 1866 by the Palmer family. The building was designed by James Edward Rogers (1838–1896), who also designed the Church of Ireland church in Skerries. Cycle to the T-junction in the centre of Rush, and turn left towards Rush Pier. On the way look for an anchor on the right, at a Y-junction. This belonged to the *John Tayleur*. In a tragedy akin to the *Titanic*, this iron-hulled clipper sank at Lambay Island on 19 January 1854. She was launched the previous October and was to the fore in marine technology. Claiming to be the largest iron vessel of her day, she weighed 1,750 tons and measured 250 feet in length. Similar to the *Titanic*, she had sealed compartments to control flooding and was operated by the White Star Line. This was her maiden voyage too. Carrying over 600 passengers and crew, she set off from Liverpool on that fateful voyage bound for Australia. Things started to go wrong from the start. Variations were noticed in the compass readings and then a gale blew up. The captain thought he was sailing due south but the ship was actually heading west towards Ireland and Lambay Island. Finally the lookout raised the alarm when he saw water breaking on the rocks in the bay, now known as Tayleur's Point. The crew tried to veer off, but the ship was difficult to control and struck the rocks. She sank as the gale persisted. Traumatic testimony from the survivors describes their attempts to escape the ship and climb the cliffs to raise the alarm. The ship had gone down on the seaward side of the island, hidden by tall cliffs from the residents of the island and mainland. Finally a rescue got underway. Nevertheless, around 300 men, women and children, many bound for a new life in Australia, lost their lives. The *Tayleur* remained undisturbed until the late 1950s when divers located her wreck.

5. Lambay Views (Fingal)

Cycle past the pier and follow the road around to the right. Shortly after you will see a martello tower behind a row of houses, and Lambay Island ahead. The road veers right again and Portrane comes into view. After passing the housing estate take the second turn on the right. The road facing will be a cul-de-sac. At the top of this road keep left heading back into the centre of town. Cycle on for about 0.5 km and just before a petrol station veer left onto Sandy Road. Soon after is the Fingal Arts Centre in St Maur's, an old RC church founded in 1760. Continue on for about 1.5 km to Rogerstown Harbour and Estuary; Rush sailing club is also situated here. The Estuary is a wetland supporting birds of international and national significance. There are many species that winter here. Of international importance are brent-geese. Of importance nationally are populations of wildfowl and waders. You could cycle straight on along the Estuary but the road surface soon deteriorates. Turning right at the Estuary, onto the Spout Road, will bring you to the R128, about 0.5 km away. At the old water mill facing you, turn left for Lusk, about 3 km away. Cycle past the railway station and across a roundabout. The old church and round tower will guide you back to your car.

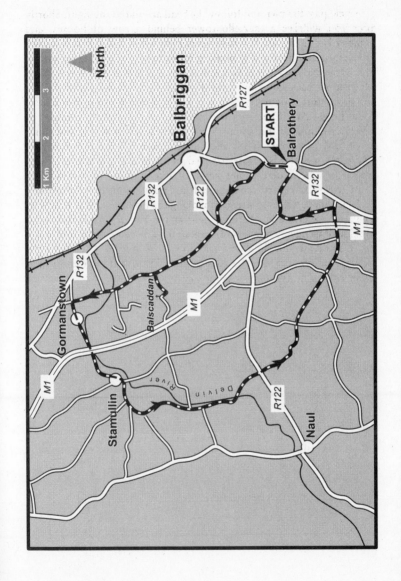

6. Balrothery–Stamullin (Fingal, Meath)

Distance (km)	22
Cycling time (hours)	$1^3/4$
Terrain	Verging on rolling
Roads (OSI 43 map)	Third-class
Attractions	River, Bog, a little Heritage

This rather easy and short route begins near the M1 motorway, ideal for a quick one. It starts at Balrothery on the old north coach road and climbs a little to Balscaddan (the town of the herrings) before descending towards Gormanstown. It was near here that St Patrick is reputed to have landed on his second visit to Ireland. The route then continues to Stamullin, founded by Moylin's son who built a monastery here, after which it passes through some very quiet and pleasant countryside near the Delvin River that borders the Fingal Meath border. Later the landscape changes to boggy ground near Ring Commons, unusual for Fingal which has some of the most fertile land in the country. Finally, sight of the ancient Norman building at Balrothery will herald your return to the 'Town of the Knights'.

Take the M1 from Dublin towards Balbriggan. Exit onto the R132 (old N1) to Balrothery and park around the village. Balrothery is about 30 km from the City.

After parking in Balrothery cycle back onto the R132 (old N1) and take the nearby turn in the direction of Balscaddan/Gormanstown. This turn is on the Balbriggan side of Balrothery on the left. After 2.5 km there is a crossroads with the R122, go straight across. The road rises towards Balscaddan about 2 km away. A slight detour left will take you into the centre of the village and to the church dedicated to Our Lady of the Assumption. Built in 1819, it cost £500 — earnestly collected from voluntary subscriptions. Balscaddan is a derivative of the Irish, meaning town of the herrings, which is a strange name for a village some distance from the sea. But apparently herrings were transported from the coast at Bremore near Balbriggan. They were prepared at Balscaddan for the Dublin market.

Return to the main road and continue descending, passing Tobersool Lane on the left. Nearby is Gormanstown Bridge over the small Delvin River. It is said that locally-born St Benignus was baptised by St Patrick in the Delvin. He went on to succeed the patron saint as Bishop of Armagh. Once you cross the river you are in the Royal County, Meath. As you cycle into the village of Gormanstown, a college of the same name, run by the Franciscan community, is on your left. A castle within the grounds was formerly the seat of the Preston family. It was built in 1786 by Sir Jenico Preston, 12th Viscount Gormanstown, on the site of a castle built in 1372. The family crest contains a fox and legend has it that when a head of the family dies foxes gather at the castle to mourn.

Continue cycling by the walls of the college and turn left just past the local shop. You will pass the college playing fields, and just beyond them is a thatched cottage on the right. Cycle over the motorway into Stamullin. There are a growing number of new housing developments in this once-small village, likely attracted by the convenience of the motorway. Stamullin was established from the site of a monastery founded by Moylin's son. As you cycle through the village note the memorial on the right to local man Sergeant Patrick Mooney and his fellow crew, who lost their lives while on a rescue mission in an Air Corps helicopter. Behind the memorial are the ruins of a church dedicated to St Patrick. There are remains of a medieval nave and chancel. Also here is the Gormanstown family vault in which a tomb cover depicts an effigy of a knight and his lady. There is also a macabre tomb cover depicting a skeleton. Cadavers such as this often show the skeleton in a state of decomposition and may have been influenced by the Black Plague that scourged the medieval period. Others remembered here are the children who died between 1952 and 1986 in St Joseph's baby home, now a nursing home in the village.

Continue on, passing St Patrick's Church on the left, founded in 1831. Just after the sign for St Clare's Nursing Home, keep left at the junction in the direction of Greenanstown and Ardcath. At the next junction about 0.5 km away turn left. It is very pleasant here as you cycle along the tree-lined road, especially when they are in their seasonal finery. After 1 km the valley of the Delvin River runs alongside you on the left. The banks of the river are bordered by trees, making it a pleasant sight. You will then cross the river, and descend a little to the crossroads at the R122, about 5 km from Stamullin. Cycle across onto another minor road in the direction of Ring Commons, about

3 km away. After 2 km you will come to a crossroads, go straight across. The road then passes through a boggy area after which is the Ring Commons Sports Centre on your right; the road veers left here. Soon you will cross over the motorway, about 5 km from the R122. Take the next left after the motorway onto a more minor road. On your right you will see a reservoir, now managed by an angling club. In the past it was used by industries in Balbriggan for generating power and cooling machinery. The road terminates at a T-Junction, turn right and pass the cricket club to Balrothery. The village was an influential centre for Norman administration, which accounts for its name, *Baile na Ridire* (town of the knights). Later in the mid-18th century, the village had a population of nearly 5,000 souls and amongst other industries produced biscuits. The biscuits were popular with the British Navy as they remained fresh over long voyages. Apparently Nelson demanded Balrothery biscuits for his fleet. And speaking of which, if you fancy a bite you could have one in the local inn before returning to your car.

7. Bachall Iosa (Fingal)

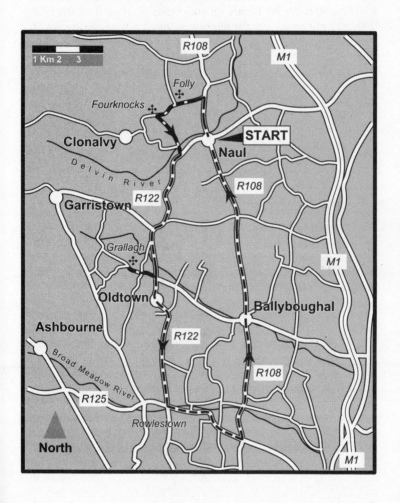

Distance (km)	37
Cycling time (hours)	4
Terrain	Hilly
Roads (osi 43 map)	All on regional except for 4 km on third-class
Attractions	Rolling countryside, Music, Heritage

The border between Fingal and Meath cuts through the Naul, and the village is surrounded by some of the highest hills in these counties. On the Meath side are magnificent views north to the Mourne Mountains, and on the Fingal side south to the Dublin mountains. South of Oldtown and Ballyboughal the terrain is quite flat.

The cycle has a hilly 2-km start from the Naul towards Fourknocks, an ancient passage tomb. The route then descends through lovely and generally open countryside to Oldtown, known as a chapel village. From here it continues to Ballyboughal, which at one time accommodated the relic Bachall Iosa or Staff of Christ. After Ballyboughal you can expect a steady climb towards the Nags Head where there are fabulous views to the south. The final section descends back to the Naul, and over coffee you can check out the cultural events happening at the Seamus Ennis Centre there.

Take the M1 north from the City and exit at the sign for Naul/Balbriggan. Turn left at the roundabout and continue to the Naul, located about 33 km from the City. Choose a place to park your car around the village centre.

Cycle north on the R108 toward Drogheda up a steep hill. Take the second left turn onto a third-class road, about 2 km from the Naul at a sign for Clonalvy. Catch your breath here and enjoy the beautiful view north to the Mourne Mountains. Look for the plaque remembering the United Irishmen of 1798 from East Meath and Fingal who fought and died for freedom. Continue on this third-class road as it rises another bit. Soon you will see a folly on your right, an eccentricity, in this case a tower topped with a balustrade. Not far from this is Fourknocks, the 'Mound on the Ground'. Actually it is a passage grave from the New Stone Age or Neolithic period. This period, from about 3,000 to 2,000 BC, is characterised by the development of agriculture and existed before the use of metal tools. The communal tomb consists of a passage leading to a chamber with three recesses off it. Unfortunately the roof is a more recent and rather unfitting development. Just inside the chamber on the left is a representation of a human face. A sign at the site indicates where a key is available to enter the tomb.

On leaving Fourknocks go left, and within 100 m turn right at a sign for Naul. Descend steeply to a stop sign at a garden centre and then turn right onto the R122 in the direction of Garristown. Cycle straight on for about 4 km to a fork junction, veer right and soon you will come to Grallagh Cemetery on the right. On the south side is a holy well located in a miniature church and probably was a popular place of pilgrimage. The well is dedicated to St Maccallin; its water is said to cure whooping cough and sore eyes. There appears to be a shamrock engraved in one of the steps down to the well, a reference to St Patrick I wonder?

Return to the R122 and continue to Oldtown, 3 km further. This is pleasant cycling with a mix of open and wooded countryside. A thatched cottage on your left will catch your eye as you cycle through the small village. It would appear that the town is not old at all in Irish terms. It is an example of a 'chapel village', which developed from widespread investment in chapel building following repeal of the penal laws. Communities grew around these chapels and the original one here, now gone, was built c. 1827. Local historian and traditional musician Patrick Archer was born in Oldtown in 1866. Much of his later life was spent recording the history and traditions of Fingal. He died in 1949.

From Oldtown continue on the R122 towards a junction with the Ashbourne/Swords road. Before this junction the road crosses the Broad Meadow River. I stopped here to watch young lambs playfully follow their mothers' lead, and pondered that soon they would be destined for someone's plate. I banished the thought, and turned left at the junction onto the R125 in the Sword's direction. Continue on this busy road through Rowlestown and finally take a left onto the R108 at the sign for Ballyboughal. The cycle to this village is across flat, open countryside and on the way you will pass Swords Open Golf Course. You could rest here while watching the players practise their golfing skills. Then continue to Ballyboughal.

A confusing thing about the name of this village is its spelling. The modern signs are written 'Ballyboughal' but the name on the old bridge there is spelt 'Ballyboghil'. Anyway the name means the Town of the Staff. It gets it from the Irish, *Bachall Iosa* or staff of Jesus. Apparently St Patrick carried the staff during his mission in Ireland and it was once kept in the old church here. Built *c.* 1113, the church is now in ruins and located just off the road on the Naul side of town. The staff, originally brought from Armagh, granted its holder a claim to be a successor to St Patrick, and was a powerful emblem of religious authority. Possibly the Norman, Strongbow, removed it from Ballyboughal to Christ Church Cathedral *c.* 1173. The staff remained there until the Reformation, when it was publicly burnt in 1538. There is a large plaque to the relic just before crossing the bridge. A 1-km detour to the left here will take you to a cenotaph remembering the Wexford men of 1798. After their defeats at Vinegar Hill and Arklow, they came north looking for support. But the weakened column was defeated decisively by the Dumfries Light Dragoons here at Drishogue Lane. Many were buried at the old church where a headstone was recently erected to their memory.

Past Ballyboughal and another golf club appears to your right, Hollywood Lakes. The road is rising here and near the Nags Head rises quite steeply. At the Nags Head crossroads, about 4 km from Ballyboughal, detour right at a sign for Lusk. At about 0.5 km, look for the cemetery and old church off the road to your right. The views south over Dublin City and Mountains are magnificent. On a clear day, you can see the stacks of Poolbeg Power Station on the Liffey. Return to the R108 and turning right you will soon descend to the sleepy village of Naul.

Naul is a place of Irish culture. There is a centre here called 'The Seamus Ennis Centre', named in honour of one of Ireland's foremost traditional musicians and broadcasters. He lived in the Naul and died in 1982. The centre is a nice place to have coffee and to check out the cultural events in store.

In days gone by the Naul was an important transport stage. The Dublin-to-Drogheda coach stopped there to change horses. The coach was drawn by four horses and on the top, called the 'Cock Roost', were seated the lower-class passengers. On parts of the journey the male passengers had to alight and push and haul the coach up steep hills and across marshy ground. Also, passengers came under threat of being robbed by highwaymen. Compared to modern transportation, these travellers had it rough and paid handsomely for their journey. The fare from Dublin to Drogheda must have been a small fortune, considering that from Church Street in Dublin to Ballymun on its outskirts was 3/4d. The average wage then was 6d a day! Isn't it grand that we can do it now on a bicycle for free?

8. THE ESTUARY CIRCUIT (FINGAL)

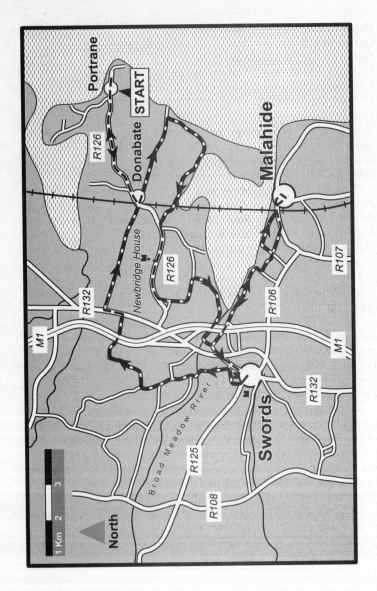

Distance (km)	50
Cycling time (hours)	$5^1/4$
Terrain	Flat
Roads (osi 43, 50 maps)	Half regional and half third-class
Attractions	Coast, Park, Bird-watching, Heritage

This is an easy cycle except for a small challenge to suit the more nimble cyclist. On a short part of the route at high tide you will have to carry your bicycle, but otherwise the going is easy. The route takes in two tidal estuaries, and is therefore one for the birdwatcher.

It starts at Portrane where there is a fine view of Lambay Island, an ornithologist's dream. Past Donabate and its numerous golf clubs, the route follows the northside of the Broad Meadow Estuary, itself a bird sanctuary. It then traces the south side to the charming town of Malahide. After which it leaves the confines of the Broad Meadow Estuary and turns towards the ancient town of Swords, founded by St Columba. After Swords the route meanders back to Portrane, but not before detouring to a bird hide on the Rogerstown Estuary, also an important bird sanctuary.

Take the M1 past the airport and exit at the turnoff for Skerries. At the second roundabout turn right for Donabate/Portrane. Drive through Donabate following the sign for Portrane Beach. In Portrane pass the hospital entrance, and just past a flat-roof building is a car park. Portrane is about 25 km from Dublin.

Once on your bicycle continue on for about 1.5 km to the end of the road. Here there is an inhabited martello tower and beautiful views of Lambay Island. Lambay is the remains of an ancient volcano. It has soaring cliffs reaching over 100 m, in stark contrast to the mainland. On the site of a 15th-century castle is a large country house designed by the eminent architect Sir Edwin Lutyens for Cecil Baring, who purchased the island in 1904. Baring, who later became Lord Revelstoke, was the founder of Baring's Bank which crashed in dramatic style when a junior trader lost £800 million or so to the ether. Lambay is a nature reserve providing a shelter for a myriad of birds and a large population of grey seals.

Return passing your car and cycle on to Donabate (R126). Near Donabate Leisure Centre is the old, redbrick, national school built in 1914, where my late mother attended. It has been tastefully integrated into a housing complex. I wonder what she would have thought of it. Just past St Patrick's Church, turn left onto a third-class road following the sign for Donabate Beach. This is the land of golfers; there are four golf courses on this section of the route. After 2 km turn right before the Waterside Hotel at the sign for Balcarrick Golf Club. Continue for another 1.5 km and then the Broad Meadow Estuary comes into view. Across the Estuary you can see the tall apartments of Malahide dominating the skyline. The road hugs the shore and I saw two curlews, who took off on my approach, sounding their loud wild note. As the road veers away from the shore it crosses under the Dublin/Belfast railway line. A little later comes a junction with the R126; turn left here. Cycle for about 1 km to Newbridge Demesne whose main entrance is on the right. This fine complex consists of 360 acres of parkland containing the 18th-century Newbridge House, and an adjacent farm depicting rural life of the time. Designed by George Semple, Newbridge House was built in 1737 for Charles Cobb, later Archbishop of Dublin. The house itself contains elaborate stucco plasterwork by Robert West. In 1760 the Archbishop's daughter-in-law, Lady Elizabeth Beresford, added a large wing to the back of the mansion. The Demesne is open to the public and opening times are seasonally dependant.

Cycle back to the Demesne exit and turn right. After 1 km look for a secluded turn to the left, take this. Shortly after you will come to a yield sign, continue straight on. Follow the road all the way to the Estuary and then turn right. If the tide is high you may have to lift your bike onto the parapet that runs parallel to the shore and above the submerged road. The alternative is to get your feet wet. Be careful as the parapet is not very wide and is really suited to the more agile. The road surfaces again after several hundred metres and you can remount. A little further, where the M1 motorway crosses the estuary, is an area where mute swans and ducks, mainly mallard, are plentiful. I saw a mallard pair with their three ducklings foraging on the shoreline as I passed by in April.

Cycle on under the motorway and soon you will meet the River Broad Meadow flowing into the Estuary. Following the river you will come to a T-junction. Turn left and cross the river, then turn left again onto Estuary Road. You will cross under the motorway again, but this time on the south side of the Estuary. Cycle across the roundabout and alongside the shore towards Malahide. Along here is an information notice describing birds of the Estuary. Some birds such as the mute swan, mallard and tufted duck prefer the inner part of the Estuary, whereas the brent-goose, shelduck and oystercatcher prefer the outer extremes.

Cycle on to pedestrian lights near the modern Yellow Walls Parish Church. Before the lights, turn left onto Yellow Walls Road. At the next lights, turn left down Sea Road. Once back on the shoreline you will see the railway viaduct ahead, originally built in 1844 on a timber structure. Pass under it, and at the next lights turn right into Malahide town centre. Note that the marina is to your left at the lights, under the arch. Malahide is one of the earliest sites of human habitation in Ireland, considered to be about 7,500 BC. Later it became an important maritime town and its position on the Estuary made it a suitable base for the occupying Norsemen and their long ships. In contrast today, Malahide is occupied by less menacing leisure craft.

At the traffic lights in the town centre, turn right and pass the neo-Gothic church of St Sylvester, built in 1837. Just past the railway station is a handsome thatched house on the right known as the Casino. After passing through a set of pedestrian lights take the first turn right, down Yellow Walls Road. Follow the road all the way through the next set of traffic lights. You now begin backtracking the inward route. Cycle to the T-junction near Yellow Walls Parish Church, and turn right towards the Estuary. Continue to the roundabout and under the motor-way to the T-junction. Now turn left towards Swords. Soon you will come to another roundabout. Cycle across this, and take the next left following the sign into Swords. Opposite the courthouse is an entrance to Swords Castle. Swords Castle is a collection of medieval buildings, constructed between the 12th and 15th centuries as a fortified palace for the archbishops of Dublin. In 1641 the Castle was chosen by the Anglo-Irish to make a stand against Cromwell. His general, Sir Charles Coote, defeated the occupants killing some 200 before they retreated. Part of the castle has been restored and work is ongoing.

Exit right through the main entrance of Swords Castle onto the R125. Take the next left past a shopping centre. You will have to dismount now, as the road is one-way. Walk the short distance to St Columba's Church of Ireland with its medieval belfry and 8th-century round tower. The round tower marks the site of an ancient abbey founded by St Columba *c.* 560 AD. St Fionan Lobhar 'the leper' was appointed first abbot. From the time of St Fionan to the Early Middle Ages, Swords was a centre for the treatment of leprosy. The abbey grew in importance and wealth. It was plundered many times during the Norse invasions from the 8th to 11th centuries. Adjacent to the round tower is a 14th-century square belfry, the remains of a medieval church. The present St Columba's was built in 1818.

Go back to the R125 and turn left. At the nearby traffic lights turn right. Follow the road around taking the second left to another set of traffic lights. Cycle through these away from the built-up area. Take the second right, just after Balheary Golf Club. This is flat, farming country. After crossing over the M1 motorway you will arrive at a junction with the busy R132 (old N1). Turn left and prepare to turn right for Portrane/Donabate, 0.5 km away. After taking the right turn you will come to a stop sign, turn left onto Turvey Avenue, a long, straight stretch of tree-lined road. After 1 km there is a sign for Rogerstown Estuary Hide. Rogerstown Estuary is of international and national importance for both its habitats and the birds they support. If you are a keen birdwatcher, it is worth the 4-km detour over rough track, although the day I visited the hide was locked. However, there is an information board there, and enquiries can be made to BirdWatch Ireland.

Return to Turvey Avenue and continue to Donabate, about 2 km. At the stop sign near the railway station, turn left. Follow the road round to the left towards Portrane and back to your car, another 3 km, before resting your weary bones.

9. The Velvet Strand (Fingal)

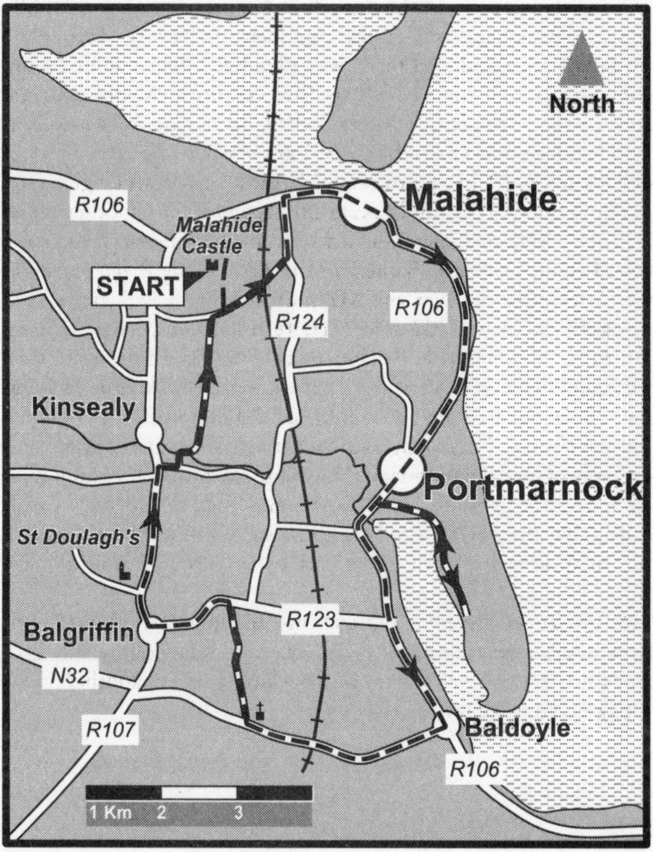

Distance (km)	24
Cycling time (hours)	$2^1/_2$
Terrain	Flat
Roads (OSI 50 map)	Two-thirds on regional, remainder on third-class
Attractions	Coast, Gardens, Bird sanctuary, Heritage

This is an easy route that in part follows scenic coastline and includes the famous Velvet Strand at Portmarnock. Traffic can be busy; however, there is a cycle lane on the busiest section. The route begins at Malahide Demesne, where there are lots to do for everyone. It passes through the town before embracing the coast to Baldoyle, passing through Portmarnock on the way. There are fine views of Lambay Island, Ireland's Eye and the peninsula of Howth on this section. At the Velvet Strand it is easy to see why it was used as a runway by early aviation pioneers. From Baldoyle Estuary you can spend time bird-watching before turning inland to busy Donaghmede on the way to the 13th-century St Doulagh's Church. At nearby Kinsealy the route takes a quiet road back to Malahide Demesne.

From the City take the M1 to the M50 interchange and turn right onto the N32 for Malahide. After 3 km turn left at the traffic lights onto the R107 to continue to Malahide. About 2 km from the town, turn right at the sign for Malahide Demesne. The entrance is a little over 0.5 km on the left. There is plenty of parking here but note opening and closing times as you enter the park. Opening time is 10 a.m. and closing time changes between 5 and 9 p.m. depending on daylight hours.

Cycle back to the Demesne main entrance and turn left for about 1 km to a stop sign. Turn left and cycle into Malahide town centre almost 1 km away. Turn right at the traffic lights onto the R106, and within a short distance in front of you is the Grand Hotel built in 1835. It became popular with Victorians who travelled from Dublin on the new railway to enjoy the benefits of the sea air and bathing. Just past the hotel the road joins the coast. Behind you is Malahide Marina, and the area across the Estuary is known as the Island, which is actually a peninsula. Behind the Island are the tall structures of Portrane, known by local fishermen as the bottles. Soon after is Hicks Tower on the right. This martello tower was converted by the architect Frederick Hicks in 1910. He cut windows and added a roof, a huge effort considering the walls are nearly 2 m thick. The next interesting building just up the road is Robswall's Castle. The Cistercian monks of St Mary's Abbey in Dublin once occupied this tower house and all fishing boats entering the harbour of Malahide gave a donation of fish to the monks. They must have been healthy men if fish and prayer was their diet. To your left is Lambay Island and ahead is the peninsula of Howth, with Ireland's Eye just off it.

You pass another inhabited martello tower and an old, conical kiosk as you enter Portmarnock, which is about 5 km from Malahide. Here the Velvet Strand is well in view, and you can see why its broad sands were used as a runway. On 24 June 1930, the 'Southern Cross' piloted by Sir Charles Kingsford Smith with navigator, Irishman Captain Paddy Saul, and two others, took off from the Velvet Strand for Newfoundland on a pioneering flight across the Atlantic from east to west. Two years later on 18 August 1932, Jim Mollison, husband of the famous woman pilot Amy Johnson, also left the Velvet Strand in his De Havilland Puss Moth aircraft, 'Heart's Content'. He was attempting to fly solo, non-stop, across the Atlantic from east to west. He landed in Newfoundland 31 hours later.

The road veers away from the coast as you enter Portmarnock. Pass St Anne's Church on the left and at the pedestrian traffic lights detour left at the sign for Portmarnock Golf Club. The Velvet Strand is also down here as is the north end of Baldoyle Estuary. Portmarnock Golf Club with its celebrated links course was founded in 1894. Its first president was John Jameson, a member of the family who founded the famous distillery in 1780. The family had been playing golf on their private course here, one of the earliest in Ireland, since 1858. The course now hosts the Irish Open. Baldoyle Estuary is the estuary of two small rivers, the Sluice and the Mayne. At low tide the exposed mudflats provide an important and protected feeding area for ducks, geese and waders. Return to the main road, R106.

After passing though Portmarnock you come to a small roundabout. Turn left here in the direction of Baldoyle, 2 km away. To your left are the wetlands of Baldoyle Estuary, to your right barren fields, and ahead is Howth Peninsula. You can also see the fine clubhouse of

Portmarnock Golf Club. In Baldoyle turn right at the Church of Ss Peter and Paul in the direction of Baldoyle Industrial Estate. The landscape here becomes rather less attractive, being built up. Turn right at the next traffic lights onto Grange Road and a cycle track. Broadstone Road is to the left. About 1.5 km from Baldoyle you will pass over the railway and soon after come to a roundabout. Just before the roundabout, on the right, are the ruins of Grange Abbey in a small park. About 1166 Dermot McMurrough gave the lands of Baldoyle to All Hallows Community. The land became a farm or grange for tenants. Grange Abbey was built in the late 13th or early 14th century to serve as a church for the tenants. Turn right at the roundabout in the direction of Balgriffin. After 1 km turn left onto the R123, and cycle another 1 km to a junction at Campion's Pub. Turn right here onto the R107 in the direction of Malahide. After 0.5 km look for St Doulagh's Church on the left. This 12th-century structure has a steep stone roof and castellated tower. A more modern church was built against the north side. St Doulagh himself was an anchorite, a hermit who lived in a cell, measuring 10 ft by 7.5 ft. Near the church is an ancient well covered by a stone structure; it may have been used as a baptismal font. St Doulagh's is open to visitors during services.

Continue for about 1.5 km and turn right at Kinsealy Church and the old national school, established in 1839. A little further on, turn left on to a peaceful road and continue for 2 km to a stop sign. Turn right here and then left back into Malahide Demesne. The 12th-century Malahide Castle and Demesne contains a coffee shop, picnic and play areas and a 9-hole golf course. Also within the Demesne are the Talbot Botanic Gardens, home to over 5,000 species of plants, the Fry Model Railway and Tara's Palace doll collection. The ruins of a medieval church stand in the grounds of the castle. Built into it are carved figures of naked women called Sheela na Gig. These date back to Celtic times and were meant to scare away evil spirits. Many Norman church builders included these figures in their buildings to deter evil and placate their new Irish parishioners. A Norman knight, Sir Richard Talbot, built the original castle around about 1200 AD. The Talbot family remained in the castle until 1976 when it transferred to the State. The castle is also associated with one of the most important literary discoveries, the Bosewell Papers. A great granddaughter of James Bosewell married the 5th Baron of Malahide in the 19th century.

Subsequently when the line of the Bosewells died out in 1917 the Bosewell papers came to Malahide Castle. However, the papers were sold to Yale University in the USA and there they reside today. It is worthwhile spending some time relaxing at Malahide Demesne and enjoying what it has to offer, before driving home.

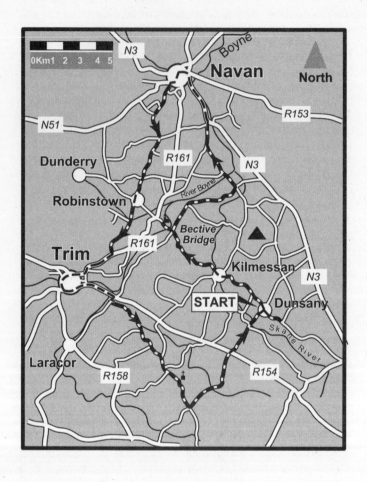

Distance (km)	57
Cycling time (hours)	6
Terrain	Rolling
Roads (osi 42 map)	Mainly third-class
Attractions	River, Woodland, plenty of Heritage

Heritage is abundant on this very pleasant route that follows in part the regal Boyne. The cycling is quite easy as the terrain just verges on rolling. The route begins at Dunsany and heads for Kilmessan where the old Navan railway line once passed. It continues to Bective Abbey, originally a 12th-century Cistercian abbey situated on a beautiful site by the banks of the Boyne. The route then follows the river to the busy market town of Navan; amongst its famous sons is Pierce Brosnan, the ice-cool 'James Bond'. After, there is a pleasant cycle through Robinstown to Trim, a heritage town containing the largest Norman castle in Europe. There is also plenty of evidence of a dynamic religious and medical past there. From Trim the route follows a tranquil and relaxing section back to Dunsany passing through small, rural communities and wooded areas.

From the City take the N3 to Dunshaughlin. In the town turn left onto the R125 towards Kilcock, and then take the first turn right following the sign for Dunsany. You can park on the left just before Dunsany Crossroads. This small community is about 34 km from the City.

Cycle back in the direction you came for about 1 km to the main entrance of Dunsany Castle, opposite is a well-weathered wayside cross. Originally built by the Norman, Hugh de Lacy, around 1180 it has been changed many times since. The castle is one of the oldest continuously-inhabited in Ireland. The Plunkett family, Lords of Dunsany, have been here since the 15th century. Within the Demesne is the 15th-century church of St Nicholas. The tombs of family members and local residents surround this fine old church. We were unable to gain access to the Demesne. Cycle back to Dunsany Crossroads and turn right, followed by left in the direction of Kilmessan, about 3 km away. In the village turn right and soon you will arrive at the Station House Hotel. This hotel is situated on a railway junction that served the old Navan line. The line, from Drogheda to Navan, was opened by the Dublin and Drogheda Railway in 1850. Its construction provided much-needed employment after the Great Famine. Over the years the success of the railway varied but Navan remained an important railhead for freight traffic until 1977, when the business was transferred to Drogheda. The track at Kilmessan was removed and the old signal box and other buildings now form part of the hotel.

Continue past the hotel towards Bective, 3.5 km away. Just before the crossroads there you will pass an unusual red house on the left. This modern building has a circular section attached, rather like a round tower of old, but shorter and broader. Go straight across at the crossroads and over the bridge to Bective Abbey. This impressive abbey-fortress overlooks the River Boyne. It was the second Cistercian abbey to be established in Ireland following Mellifont. Founded *c.* 1150 by the King of Meath, it was one of the most important monastic sites in the country. The Abbot of Bective sat in the Parliament of the Pale and those turbulent times are the reason for its defensive reconstruction around the 15th century. The abbey was closed in 1536 by Henry VIII in his bid to control the wealth and power of the Catholic Church. It was later turned into a great mansion and modified again to suit the new residents.

Return to the crossroads and turn left. After 4.5 km there is another crossroads, turn left again in the direction of Navan. After crossing the Boyne you will cycle by pleasant woodland on the right. Continue past a school, following the sign for Navan, about 5 km. Soon after you will come to a junction with the busy N3. There is a Chinese restaurant on the left. Turn left and as you cycle towards Navan the Boyne is to your right. Cross under the arched, railway bridge and cycle on until you see the offices of the *Meath Chronicle*. Turn left here into the town centre. After a short distance you will need to dismount and walk through the town, as the road system is one-way. This is a lively modern town with plenty of places to replenish. The town boasts of several famous offspring. Amongst them are Sir Francis Beaufort (1774–1856), the Royal Navy admiral who created the Beaufort Scale for wind force, and more recently Pierce Brosnan, the actor who played a slick 007, 'James Bond', the agent who sorts out those international villains.

Having walked through the town centre you will come to a set of traffic lights. You can remount your bicycle and cycle straight on in the direction of Athboy (N51). After 0.5 km veer left at Pairc Tailteann, the GAA grounds. A hospital is on the opposite side. Cycle on in the direction of Robinstown, about 7 km away. This is a pleasant cycle on a third-class road, once you have left the confines of Navan. At Robinstown turn right and then left for Trim, 6 km. About 2 km from Robinstown you will pass a small airfield on the left. Soon after you meet with the R161. Turn right here in the direction of Trim, 4 km away.

Trim or *Baile Atha Troim* means the town of the ford of the elder tree, and is a heritage town. As you cycle into town the clock on the belfry of St Patrick's Cathedral is to your right. Trim Castle, sometimes known as King John's Castle, is in the centre of town. This imposing fortress was built by the Anglo-Norman Hugh de Lacy *c.* 1173 and was a powerful emblem of Norman power. It has a fine square keep. A moat encircled the walls, which could be filled from the Boyne if enemy threatened. Left of the main gate, whilst facing it, is the Yellow Steeple with its massive arched window near the top. This 14th-century bell tower is all that remains of the Priory of St Mary's, an Augustine house. It was badly damaged during the wars of the 17th century. After leaving the castle continue through the town to the Wellington Column. The Duke of Wellington, Sir Arthur Wellesley, was educated locally. The townspeople erected the column after his success at Waterloo. Turn left at the traffic lights here, followed soon after by another left. Once at the roundabout turn right onto the R154 in the direction of Clonee/Dublin. About 1 km from Trim town centre you will see the Priory of St John the Baptist. The Bishop of Meath, Simon de Rochfort, founded this facility in the 13th century for the Fratres Cruciferi or the Crutched Friars. It was here that they cared for the sick. Cycle on, and nearby are the Newtown Monuments, accessed by crossing a narrow bridge controlled by traffic lights. This religious site was also founded by Simon de Rochfort and consists of a medieval cathedral, two monasteries and a small church. There is also a 16th-century altar tomb on which are the effigies of Sir Luke Dillon and his wife.

Return to the main road and continue for about 2 km to a crossroads at Jack Quinn's Pub. Jack Quinn was one of three brothers who were famous Meath footballers nearly 40 years ago. Jack had a reputation for scaring the opposition and won an All-Ireland medal in 1967. Turn right at the pub onto a third-class road and next left. Cycle for about 5 km along a quiet country road until you come to an old church built in 1880, and surrounded by yew trees. Just past the church turn left following the sign for Kilcock and cycle for about 2 km to a crossroads. Turn left at the pub here following the sign for Dunsany. Continue for about 4 km to the junction with the R154. Cycle straight across and on to Dunsany, another 3 km, where you can return to your car and prepare for home. Unfortunately there is no eating or drinking enterprise here, so one must lick one's lips in anticipation of later treats.

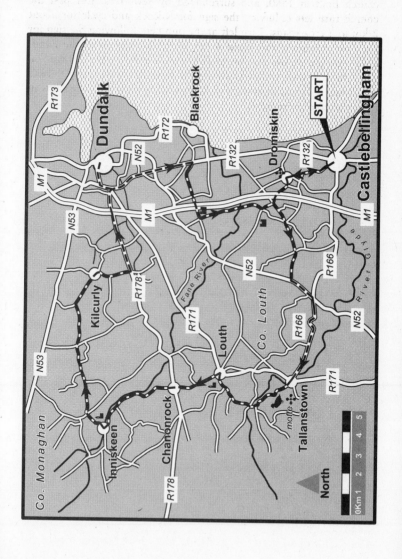

Distance (km)	67
Cycling time (hours)	6
Terrain	Rolling
Roads (OSI 36 map)	Three-quarters on third-class, remainder on regional
Attractions	Pretty villages, Rivers, Bird sanctuary, Heritage

This cycle follows a route around north Louth which has a legacy of ancient monasteries, and dips into County Monaghan to find the roots of the contemporary poet, Patrick Kavanagh. Overall the terrain is rolling and not too taxing. The route begins in Castlebellingham and heads north towards Dromiskin, once an important ecclesiastical centre from the time of St Patrick. It then turns west to picturesque Tallanstown, a prize-winner in the National Tidy Towns competition. From there the route turns north again to Louth, another ancient and holy place. It continues north to cross the Monaghan border into Inniskeen which celebrates a former son and famous poet. The village is also the site of an ancient monastery. After, the route turns eastward to the busy urban centre of Dundalk, with its magnificent Procathedral. After Dundalk the return follows rural byways back to Dromiskin and Castlebellingham.

From Dublin, take the M1 past the exit for Ardee. Take the next exit onto the R166, following the signs for Castlebellingham, which is about 72 km from Dublin. You should find parking around the town centre.

Cycle back up town in the direction you drove in and straight past the junction with the road (R166) you came in on. You are heading to Dromiskin about 3 km away. In the village centre of Dromiskin turn right at the sign for the round tower. Here you will find in a cemetery the truncated ruins of a round tower and two churches, one of which is 19th-century, the other probably medieval. This place was an important religious site from St Patrick's time and was possibly founded by his disciple Lughaidh. According to Celtic legend, St Ronan cursed the king of Dal Araidhe, Suibhne Geilt, to madness, for interfering with the building of his church. St Ronan became abbot here but died of the plague *c.* 660 AD, and no wonder after what he did to Suibhne. The monastic settlement was later plundered by Norsemen from nearby Annagassan. Eventually the monks left and took refuge in St Mochta's at Louth. On the day I was here, a generous local man interrupted his prayerful vigil at a graveside to show me the marks of what is customarily called a crow's foot. It is located on the bottom part of an ancient doorway to the 19th-century church. He informed me that this was the tidemark for when the sea once flooded the area.

Return to the main road and cycle directly across. Continue past St Peter's Church on the left. Soon after you will pass over the M1 motorway and at the next crossroads turn left at the sign for Ardee and the N52. Cycle to the junction with the N52, about 6 km from Dromiskin. Turn left onto the N52 and continue for about 1 km to a pub called the Glyde Inn, turn right here onto the R166 towards Tallanstown. The 4 km or so of road to Tallanstown is undulating, like you were cycling on the back of a giant serpent. As you arrive into the village turn left onto the R171, and cross the River Glyde into the centre. This is a pretty village that won a National Tidy Towns prize. At the centre turn right passing by a motte on the left. Here also is Maguire Park, a bird sanctuary. As you cycle, the River Glyde is to your right for a few hundred metres before veering away. But about 2.5 km from Tallanstown you will cross the River Glyde again and after the crossing there is an S-bend. Veer right at a Y-junction just after. About 2 km further will take you to a yield sign. Take the second right here in the direction of Louth, a place, they say, that was once a temple to the Celtic god Lugh.

At the village green and before the old water pump is a track that will take you to St Mochta's House and St Mary's Abbey. St Mochta's House is the smaller, imposing, stone building on the left. St Mochta was a disciple of St Patrick and founded a monastery here around the 6th century. His house or oratory may have originated from the middle of the 9th century, and was built to withstand the fires started by plundering Norsemen to burn monks out of their monasteries. It was certainly made to last and has seen many an invader away over the last thousand years or so. St Mary's Abbey has not been so fortunate — founded later, the present ruins are a reconstruction in 1312 after a fire. However, records and evidence of Romanesque decorations suggest that the abbey was also developed earlier through the patronage of the King of Oriel and the Bishop of Louth. Like many abbeys in Ireland, St Mary's was suppressed during the Reformation and destroyed following the rebellion of 1641.

Return to the main road and after the pump turn left at the sign indicating Inniskeen. After 3 km you will come to the junction with the R178, cycle directly across following the sign for Inniskeen, 5 km away. After 1 km or so the road passes by the Fane River, which marks the Louth/Monaghan border, for a while before crossing into Monaghan to Inniskeen. The village too is famous for its ecclesiastical tradition and more recently for the shoemaker, farmer and poet, Patrick Kavanagh, who was born nearby in 1904. After leaving primary school, Kavanagh followed his father's footsteps as shoemaker and farmer. His first book of poetry, *Ploughman and Other Poems*, was published in 1936. He then became increasingly dissatisfied with life as a small farmer. In 1938 he left Inniskeen, finally settled in Dublin and became known in the literary world as 'The Ploughman Poet'. His epic poem 'The Great Hunger' was published in 1942. In 1954 he was diagnosed with lung cancer. While recovering from an operation Kavanagh rediscovered his poetic creativity, and a new phase began after which he received the acclaim he deserved. Patrick Kavanagh died in Dublin in 1967. As you enter the village, the Patrick Kavanagh Centre is in an old church to your left.

Continue into the village and turn right towards the round tower and Fane River. Only a stub remains of the original round tower, part of a monastery founded by St Daig McCarell *c.* 7th century. There are some picnic tables nearby on the banks of the Fane River, a pleasant place to stop and replenish. Continue on towards Dundalk cycling under an old railway bridge to a crossroads about 1 km away. Cycle straight across. The road rises towards the next crossroads about 3.5 km further and offers some views of the Cooley Mountains located north of Dundalk. Continue through the crossroads in the direction of Kilcurly, 4 km away. After 2 km fork right onto a minor road at a Y-junction. At Kilcurly follow the road around to the right towards the R178, about 2 km away. At the junction with the R178, turn left at the sign for Dundalk, 5 km. This is the Dundalk–Carrickmacross road and is quite busy.

Dundalk gets its name from Cuchulainn's fort, Dun Dealgan, and has been a busy urban centre since the Norman conquest of the

12th century. As you approach Dundalk, cross over the Western Bypass, under construction on the day I passed. Follow the signs for the town centre passing by a church on the left called the Friary, so a local told me. Continue onto the one-way system coming into Market Square. Cycle past the courthouse and the magnificent Procathedral comes into view. Keep to the right passing the front of the Cathedral and continue uptown towards Dublin. Continue through the town and pass the Dundalk Institute of Technology, on your left about 3 km from the town centre. Then cycle through the nearby traffic lights onto the R132 (old N1) towards Castlebellingham. At the next traffic lights there is a short stretch of cycling lane. About 3 km from the Institute of Technology, turn right at a staggered crossroads by Sexton's Pub onto a minor road in the direction of Burn's Cottage. The cycling becomes more pleasant now as the traffic noise diminishes behind you. Continue to cycle, through a crossroads and under the railway and M1 motorway bridges, for about 3 km from the R132. At the next cross-roads nearby turn left and note the old castle in a field on your left, probably a 15th-century tower house. These buildings were designed as fortified dwellings consisting of a tall, square-type tower surrounded by a courtyard. Today the courtyards are missing generally. Follow the road for about 3.5 km to a stop sign and note another tower house on the right, in this case in a farmyard. Turn left here to the crossroads less than 1 km away and continue straight on towards Dromiskin, about 1.5 km further. Soon you will pass over the motorway and rail-way before finally entering the village. In the village centre turn right in the direction of Castlebellingham, 3 km away, back-tracking the road you started out on. There are a number of establishments in Castlebellingham, including the historic Bellingham Castle Hotel, if you feel like something to eat and drink before returning to your car.

12. Holy Crosses and Haunted Castles (Meath, Fingal)

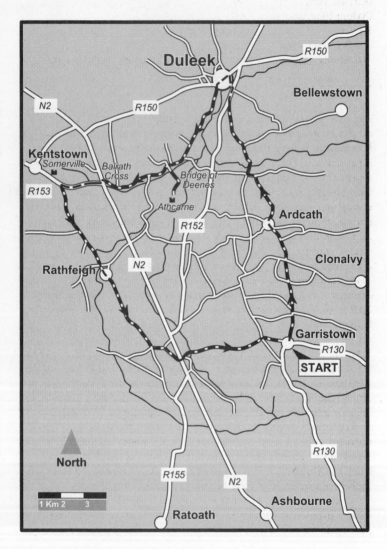

12. Holy Crosses and Haunted Castles (Meath, Fingal)

Distance (km)	40
Cycling time (hours)	$4^3/4$
Terrain	Mainly rolling
Roads (OSI 43 map)	Third-class
Attractions	Rolling countryside, Rivers, Haunted castle, Heritage

You can experience the rural charm around the Fingal/Meath border on this route, and explore the southern features of the Royal County. It is hard to believe that you are so near Dublin and yet there is such rural serenity. The cycle is quite easy going across gentle undulations except for a testing ascent on the last few kilometres returning to Garristown. It begins at Garristown where the curious Fingal Charabanc once chugged through. It then passes Ardcath and a burial mound, from which grand views of the surrounding countryside can be seen. Continuing to the historic town of Duleek, you can follow the closing stages of the Battle of the Boyne and see images of Duleek's impressive Christian past. Nearby, experience an unusual sight — two rivers confluence beside the Bridge of the Deenes. Afterwards, visit a haunted castle and then continue through the quiet village of Rathfeigh, eventually returning across the county border to Garristown.

Take the N2 from the City, eventually passing under the M50. About 6.5 km from the motorway turn right onto the R130 for Garristown. Continue to the village, about 27 km from the City. Park your car around the village centre. As you stand there taking in the surroundings, imagine a hybrid vehicle, a combination of motorbus and stagecoach, parked near the church. This was the Fingal Charabanc, a service operated by the Fingal Motor Transport Company in the 1920s, and 'providing a service to Dublin from the most inaccessible district of the county of Dublin'. It was a most curious sight as it chugged to its stop in the main street. The cycle begins around this stop.

Cycle on through Garristown towards Ardcath. As you leave the village, over to the left are the ruins of a medieval church that you will pass again on your return. About 2 km from the village is the border into County Meath. Look to the right for a ruined windmill. Flour windmills were quite common around the area in the 18th century. Factors that influenced their development were the availability of local cereal, limited water supplies and favourable winds. However, strong winds often led to their destruction. Continue to Ardcath, and at the pub detour left for about 1 km to a crossroads. On the left is an ancient unexcavated burial mound. The views from here to the north are quite spectacular.

Return to Ardcath and turn left in the direction of Duleek. Continue to follow the signs for the village to the second junction that indicates Duleek is 4 km, turn right in the direction of the sign. Continue through the next junction and enjoy the pleasant views as you go. Approaching Duleek, the smoking stacks of the cement factory can be seen in the distance. Soon you will arrive at the junction for the R152, turn right here and then left. As you enter Duleek you come to a bridge over the River Nanny. This is where the Jacobite forces retreated after the Battle of the Boyne (route 27). Although beaten that day their losses were few and they managed to regroup. However, they suffered a fatal defeat at Aughrim a year later. Cross over the bridge into the village and turn left. St Patrick is thought to have founded a monastery here in the 5th century. He left St Cianan, colloquial Keenan, after him to administer in the community. The church built then was one of the first in Ireland to be of stone rather than wood; nothing of it remains today. But Duleek is named after *damh liag*, church of stone. Turn right at the village green for the old church and high crosses. The remains here are of St Mary's, originally an Augustinian priory. Inside are interesting tombstones from the 17th century as well as high crosses depicting biblical scenes thought to date back to the 10th century. Note the great tree planted on the village green as you return to the main street. This is a lime tree, one of the oldest in Ireland and not native to the country. The people of Duleek, in memory of the union of William of Orange and his wife Mary, planted this tree along with an ash. The ash has long since gone but the lime, representing William, still remains.

Continue through the village and you will come to another green with a wayside cross set on a pedestal. This was erected *c.* 1601 by Genet Dowdall in memory of her husband William Bathe of Athcarne. At the junction here take the road to Trim. About 2.5 km from Duleek is a memorial to the insurgents of 1798. You can detour left here for about 0.5 km to the Bridge of the Deenes, an ancient bridge under which two rivers confluence, the Nanny and the Hurley. Return to the main road and cycle on to the next junction about 1 km further. Here you will find another wayside cross, dedicated to Sir Luke Bathe and erected *c.* 1675 by his wife Dame Cecilia Dowdall. She lived in nearby Athcarne Castle. Across the road you can take the side road to the ruin of this castle, about a 2-km detour. This is a remarkable Elizabethan, fortified mansion, originally built *c.* 1587. It is reputed to be haunted. The wails of dying soldiers are supposed to have been heard here, along with the ghost of a young girl whose hands drip with blood. A creepy place, it's probably best to avoid at midnight!

Return to the main road and cycle on for about 2.5 km to the junction of the busy N2 at Balrath Cross. Opposite the post office here is yet another wayside cross. This one is older than the others, but like them presents biblical scenes. Apparently 35 wayside crosses have been recorded in Meath. Turn right onto the N2 and immediate left onto the R153 in the direction of Kentstown. After 1.5 km and near a petrol station you will see the grand Somerville House away off to your right, a private residence. A family of the same name owned it once. Shortly after turn left onto a third-class road for Rathfeigh about 4 km cycle. There is a processing plant beside the junction. You will pass through a small deciduous forest. As you approach Rathfeigh the route passes over the River Hurley. Rathfeigh is a compact community and a short detour left will bring you to the local church, beside which is a handsome thatched house.

Return to the main road and continue on through farmland evidenced by the strong agricultural odours, and enjoy some fine views over the rolling countryside. About 3 km from Rathfeigh turn left at a crossroads. Soon you will come to the Snailbox Pub, turn right here at the sign for Garristown, 9 km away. The route descends to a junction with the N2. Cross the N2 following the signs for Garristown. The road now rises quite steeply over 4 km, from 80 to 135 m. Near Garristown you will descend into the village passing a medieval church on your right. The tithes from this church belonged to the Order of the St John of Jerusalem at Kilmainham. In 1302 the value of the tithe was £20 of which £2 went to the pope. With that medieval financial transaction in mind, continue past the church and turn right back to your car.

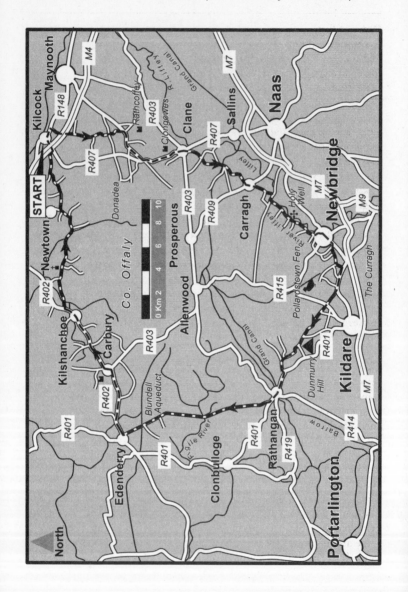

13. The Bog Circuit (Kildare, Offaly)

Distance (km)	95
Cycling time (hours)	7¹/₄
Terrain	Flat (mostly)
Roads (osi 49, 55 maps)	Mostly third-class
Attractions	Bog, Rivers, Canal, Heritage

This, the longest route in the book, crosses the contrasting environment of County Kildare; lush countryside, desolate bog and the gaping Curragh landscape. Although covering a little of some other routes in the area, it still manages to explore new territory, even a little of County Offaly. Overall the terrain is flat except for some hilly ground approaching Rathangan and Kilcock.

The route begins at Kilcock and heads through lush countryside to Clane and then on to the busy town of Newbridge. Crossing the exposed landscape of the Curragh, it passes by the Curragh Racecourse towards Rathangan, a quiet town on the Grand Canal and Slate River. After Rathangan the terrain changes again as evidenced by the drying turf, laid in strips and mounds, on the ancient bog. The bog road leads into County Offaly and the town of Edenderry near the source of the historic River Boyne. Finally the route returns via Carbury to Kilcock through lush countryside once more.

Take the N4/M4 past Maynooth and exit for Kilcock. Follow the signs into town. You should find parking around the town centre, and the Square in particular. Kilcock is about 34 km from Dublin City.

Once on your bicycle, cross over the canal and railway line towards the Fair Green. Turn immediate left after crossing the railway into the Fair Green and follow the road along the railway line. After 1 km the road takes a sharp right away from the railway. Continue for 1.5 km before crossing over the M4 motorway. Another 1 km and the road bends sharply to the left, turn immediate right after the bend. After 3 km you come to a crossroads; go straight across. Cycle for another 1.5 km to a yield sign at a junction with the R408. Turn right and then the road veers right towards Rathcoffey, about 1 km away. Here are the ruins of Rathcoffey Castle. The lands of Rathcoffey were granted to Sir John Wogan in 1317 as a reward for his family's service to the English crown. The Wogans continued to thrive until the 18th century when John Wogan died without an heir. Rathcoffey was then inherited by the Talbot family. They sold it in the late 1700s to Archibald Hamilton Rowan who demolished much of the castle in order to build a house. I am told that there is little remaining today; I was unable to witness this myself for when I passed an uninviting sign indicated that trespassers would be prosecuted. There is also a large animal feed and fertiliser company located at Rathcoffey, the factory building towering over the village.

Continue on the R408 following the sign for Prosperous. After 2 km there is a stop sign at a junction with the R407, turn left following the sign for Clane, 4 km away. About 1 km further is a fine castellated entrance that opens the long avenue to Clongowes Wood College. Originally known as Castle Browne, the Jesuits obtained the property in 1814 in somewhat controversial circumstances. At the time a number of prominent people regarded the development as putting Ireland in imminent danger of 'popish treachery'. Some things never change! However, the college survived and continues to educate young gentlemen today. One of its more famous scholars was James Joyce who reflected his experiences in boarding school in *A Portrait of the Artist as a Young Man*.

Cycle on to Clane about 2 km away. This busy town near the River Liffey was visited by St Patrick who blessed a well here known as Sunday's Well, as it was traditionally visited on that day. Near the centre of Clane turn right into town. After the turn for Prosperous and just past the Corner House Pub, turn right again. A little over 1 km from Clane you come to a crossroads, go straight across. Continue another 2 km to the lazy waters of the Grand Canal. Cross over and continue straight on for 3 km until you meet the R409. Turn left onto the R409 to the village of Carragh a short distance away. Note the church when entering the village. It has a fine portico belfry with two smaller ones on each side. Turn right just past the church following the sign for Newbridge, 9 km away. Soon you cross over the main railway line to the south and after another 1 km you come to a T-junction with a thatched cottage facing you. Turn right in the direction of Newbridge, 7 km. Take the next left continuing to follow the signs for Newbridge. About 1 km further you pass a cemetery with a holy well inside. A grotto was recently built by the local community over the

13. The Bog Circuit (Kildare, Offaly)

well, which is dedicated to St Patrick. People leave their petitions at the feet of the patron saint's effigy. It is a pleasant place to sit quietly and reflect before moving on. And when you move on, occasionally the River Liffey licks the edge of the road while you make your way to Newbridge, about 5 km away. This busy town developed from the British cavalry barracks established here in 1816. Lord Cardigan, who led the disastrous charge of the Light Brigade in the Crimea in 1854, was stationed here. Today Newbridge is influenced by the Curragh military camp nearby and has also grown into a large commuter town.

On entering Newbridge you come to a T-junction. Turn left to bring you towards the town centre. At the next T-junction with the busy R445 and beside the Liffey, turn right into the town centre. Cycle through Newbridge until you see a Ford garage on your right. Turn right at the garage and veer left. Continue a short distance to an old church, St Patrick's, dating from *c*. 1828. Keep right of the church and cycle on through a set of traffic lights into open country. Pass the turn for Pollardstown Fen and in less than 1 km you come to a junction with the R413 — opposite is a large effigy of the filly Ridgewood Pearl. Turn right and pass the Curragh Racecourse where the gaping plains of the Curragh landscape dominate. About 2 km from Ridgewood Pearl are two turns to the right. Take the second one following the sign for Rathangan. Mind the sheep as they can waddle across the road in an instant. After 2 km you come to a staggered crossroads with the busy R415. Cycle across onto the third-class road opposite, following the sign for Rathangan. After 4 km the road rises near Dunmurry Hill, which will be to your left. When you pass a left V-turn soon after, the view stretches over wide open landscape. Continue following the road for about 4 km to Rathangan, passing over the Grand Canal and Slate River on entering the town. In the centre of town turn left, and continue to a Y-junction. Keep right following the sign for Edenderry. On the outskirts of town there are two roads to Edenderry, take the shorter one to the right, about 13 km away.

Now the route takes you into bog country, marked by a Bord na Mona depot outside Rathangan. Although the bog looks quite desolate it is abundant in flora. One of the more bizarre is the carnivorous plant. Several species have developed the ability to trap and eat insects to supplement the meagre diet available on the bog. Amongst them, the round-leaved sundew is a small carnivorous plant that grows in and around bog pools. It has reddish leaves covered in hairs that produce a sticky substance which attracts insects. Unfortunately for the insects they get trapped on the gluey tentacles. The leaf then slowly closes over the struggling victim and the soft parts of the insect's body are digested by the plant over a day or two. So while on the bog be mindful of what you poke.

Typical of bog roads, the one here is fairly straight for miles ahead and ripples with undulating consistency. About halfway to Edenderry you pass over the Figile River marking the border with County Offaly. About 2 km from Edenderry is the Blundell Aqueduct crossing the Grand Canal, and then you enter the outskirts of the town. Close to the centre is a junction with the R402. Turn left onto this road into town. Edenderry is a busy place situated on a spur of the Grand Canal appropriately called the Edenderry Branch. The town gets its name from a great oak wood that was nearby until the 20th century. Although stretching back to the Middle Ages, modern Edenderry developed with the building of the canal from the early 19th century.

Return to the junction where you entered the town but cycle straight on in the direction of Dublin. This road will also take you to Carbury, about 6 km away. Near the village you come to a junction with the R403, turn left. In the centre of Carbury keep right following the main road to Dublin. The ruins that can be seen at the side of Carbury Hill are of a great Tudor mansion built by the Colleys. Another 6 km will take you to the village of Kilshanchoe. Take the first turn right after passing through the village onto a third-class road. After 1 km you cross over the curiously named Fear English River. Continue a further 2 km to a stop sign and turn right for about 1 km to a crossroads. On the left in a cemetery are the ruins of Dunfierth Church. It contains a mortuary chapel enclosing the effigy and tomb of Sir Walter Bermingham who died in 1548.

Continue straight on through the crossroads for about 4 km where you will pass over the River Blackwater and arrive at a junction by Knockanally Golf Club. At the stop sign go straight on. The road ascends about 50 m over 1.5 km. On the descent, take the turn to the right just after one to the left. Don't miss it by speeding by or else you will end in Newtown. After you take the right turn, the village of Newtown will be on your left. Follow the road for about 6 km to a

13. The Bog Circuit (Kildare, Offaly)

stop sign, and then turn left for Kilcock, 1 km away. Cross over the M4 and turn left off the roundabout towards town. Finally cross the railway and canal back into town, and to your car. Having just traversed bog roads, it's appropriate to mention that Teresa Brayton, author of the nostalgic *The Old Bog Road*, was born near Kilcock in 1868.

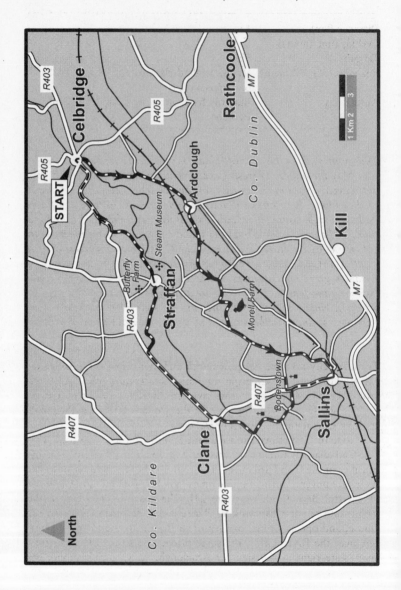

Distance (km)	51
Cycling time (hours)	5
Terrain	Flat
Roads (osi 49, 50 maps)	Mainly on third-class, except for about 5 km on regional roads
Attractions	Butterfly farm, Steam museum, River, Canal, Heritage

The countryside in this part of Kildare is very fertile, and when I cycled it in May the images of fresh growth made the experience very pleasant indeed. The route is an easy one and characteristic of the flatness of the county. It begins in Celbridge which claims to have the finest Palladian-style house in Ireland. After, it follows the River Liffey for a time on the way to Ardclough. From here the quiet roads meander to Sallins, set by the tranquil waters of the Grand Canal. The route then heads for Clane where nearby Bodenstown contains the tomb of Ireland's great revolutionary Wolfe Tone. Continuing on, the route passes by the famous K Club before arriving at the tranquil village of Straffan. Finally it turns in a direction for Celbridge, but not before passing a steam museum situated in a pleasant rural environment on the way.

From the city take the N4 past Lucan and then exit for Celbridge on the R403 (about 22 km from the City), the town is well signposted from here. In Celbridge, cross over the bridge and turn right to Castletown House. You can park in the grounds here near the solid-looking Christchurch Church of Ireland.

Cycle to Castletown House about 800 m from the entrance. This fine Palladian-style mansion was built *c.* 1722 for William Conolly, Speaker of the Irish Parliament. The Conollys built a number of follies to relieve poverty during famine times, notably Conolly's Folly and the Wonderful Barn (both on route 21). The grounds are open to the public and popular for walking. There is an admission charge to the house, and opening times are seasonal. Return to the town and turn left over the River Liffey, the same bridge you drove over, but turn immediate right at the sign for Ardclough. As you cycle along, the

Liffey is to your right. On the outskirts of Celbridge the well-kept gardens are mature, with varieties of trees and shrubs pleasing to the eye, in May anyway. About 3 km from Celbridge you come to a series of sharp bends and junctions, stay on the main road. About 1.5 km further and on a narrow bridge you pass over the railway to Dublin. Another 1.5 km will take you into Ardclough.

At a junction near the church continue straight on in the direction of Straffan. On the day I was here the signs were wrong as the sign for Kill was pointing towards Straffan. About 1.5 km from Ardclough, you will pass over the railway line again, and afterwards the road becomes bordered by trees. Emerging through them you come to a junction, turn left. At the next junction less than 1 km away, turn right onto the minor road. Continue over the little Morell River and at the next junction turn left. Soon you will see Morell Farm on the left, which is open to the public. Just past the farm is a bad bend to the right. There is a T-junction about 1 km past the farm, turn left at the stop sign. Continue on this road for about 5 km to Sallins, passing a crossroads with Killeen Golf Club signposted to the left. As you approach Sallins expect a gradual incline before finally descending into the village. On entering the village the Grand Canal appears to your left, with tied-up barges lining its banks. Once it provided services to passengers on the canal, now the village is popular with fishermen and tourists, and it's equipped with a number of establishments for food and drink.

Turn right onto the busy R407 in the direction of Clane. About 1.5 km from Sallins, pass the sign for Millicent Golf Club and take the nearby turn to the right, following the sign for Bodenstown Cemetery. Wolfe Tone's grave is here, about 0.5 km from the turn. Theobald Wolfe Tone was born in 1763 and became one of Ireland's greatest celebrated patriots. He was born into a well-to-do family and qualified as a lawyer, after which he got involved in politics. Tone was a founder member of the United Irishmen, a society originally established in Belfast in 1791. The radical movement, which was influenced by political events in Europe and contained people of various religious persuasions, demanded separation from England. Tone later organised several ill-fated, French-supported expeditions to help overthrow the English. Unfortunately his last one saw him captured off Donegal in 1798. He was convicted of treason but rather than giving the authorities the satisfaction of hanging him, he committed suicide. Wolfe Tone's legacy was to turn the disastrous 1798 Rebellion into a heroic struggle for future Irish revolutionaries.

Return to the R407 and turn left back towards the sign for Millicent Golf Club. Turn right at the sign and soon you will cross the River Liffey. On the day I passed I watched a fly fishermen skilfully toss his line to flow with the current. I did not wait around to see if he caught anything, but there was determination in his actions. About 1.5 km from the river you will pass the elegant Church of St Michael and All Angels. This was built *c.* 1883 and has a beautiful blue clock-face with gold numerals built into the belfry. Shortly after the church, turn right. At the Y-junction, beyond the sign for Millicent Golf Club, keep left for Clane. Clane is an ancient place and legend has it that Queen Baun was so distressed by the sight of her husband's head, severed in battle, that she herself collapsed and died. As you approach the town the bell tower of an old church comes into view. This is the location of a monastery founded by St Ailbe *c.* 527, and in 1162 hosted the Synod of Clane.

Turn left onto the R407 and cycle through the town centre to the top, where the road veers right towards Celbridge, the R403. On leaving town you will cross a roundabout and then the road becomes rather boring, as it lies ahead in a straight line. After 3 km you come to a crossroads, turn right onto a third-class road and get relief from the traffic. Soon you come to a sharp left bend, followed by another to the right. About 1 km later is the entrance to the Kildare Hotel and Country Club or the K Club, on the right. Originally called Straffan House and built by Hugh Barton in 1832, it is set amongst 550 acres of manicured grounds. It is now a luxurious hotel with world-class golfing facilities. In September 2006, the K Club will host the 36th Ryder Cup on the Arnold Palmer-designed course. Having soaked up the opulence here, continue to the nearby village of Straffan. Taking a 1-km detour at the Church of Ireland church will take you to the Butterfly Farm, opened June to August. There is a large exhibition of butterfly collections from around the world. You can enjoy colourful blooms and exotic plants while the butterflies fly around you.

Return to the town and at the RC church turn right onto a minor road for the Steam Museum on the right. This is open during the summer months, and contains working steam engines set in an 18th-century walled garden. Cycle on for about 2 km to the R403.

Another 2 km will take you to the outskirts of Celbridge where you will turn right towards the town centre. On the way in on the right is Celbridge Abbey, built *c.* 1697 by Bartholomew Vanhomrigh, Lord Mayor of Dublin. His daughter Vanessa had romantic attachments with Dean Jonathan Swift of *Gulliver's Travels* fame. The Abbey is currently owned by the St John of God Order. Normally the grounds are open to the public, but on the day I passed a notice announced that the grounds had to be closed because of unsocial behaviour. Opposite is Oakley Park, formerly Celbridge House. It was built in 1724 by Arthur Price when he was vicar of Celbridge. The house is thought to have been designed by the architect Thomas Burgh and like Celbridge Abbey is under the ownership of the St John of God Order. Continue on through the town to Castletown House and your car, or stop on the way at one of the many establishments if you fancy a snack.

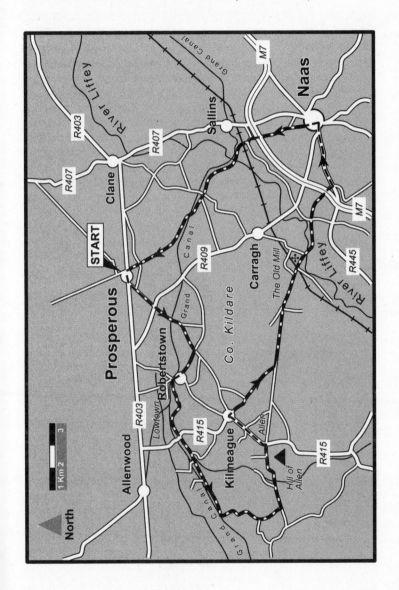

15. Grand Canal System (Kildare)

Distance (km)	45
Cycling time (hours)	$4^1/_2$
Terrain	Flat
Roads (OSI 49, 55 maps)	Mostly third-class
Attractions	Canals, River, Woodland, some Heritage

In the main this cycle follows flat terrain in the vicinity of the tranquil Grand Canal system. Starting at Prosperous the route connects with the canal in Robertstown, a picturesque village that grew with the development of the waterway. It then follows that part of the canal system known as the Barrow Line before veering away through pleasant wooded area and bog toward the Hill of Allen, where the legendary Fionn Mac Cumhaill was once based. The route then detours through the village of Kilmeague before continuing to the county town of Naas. At Naas it takes up the Grand Canal again and follows it crossing the River Liffey on the Leinster Aqueduct, a marvellous piece of 18th-century engineering. The cycle along this section is relaxing and there are opportunities to see wildlife such as swans and herons. Eventually the route turns away from the canal before finally finishing back in Prosperous.

From the city take the N4 past Lucan and then exit for Celbridge (R403). Continue through Celbridge to Clane and follow the signposts through Clane to Prosperous. There is plenty of parking just past the church in Prosperous. The village is about 37 km from the City.

Once on your bicycle, continue on the R403 and turn left just before the Maxol petrol station on the edge of the village. There is a sign here indicating the North Kildare Tourist Route. Cycle for about 4 km to the second crossroads, passing over the Grand Canal on the way. Turn right for Robertstown, another 1 km. On the day we were here the sign for Robertstown was pointing in the wrong direction. As you enter the village, the former Grand Canal Hotel is on the left with the canal facing. The Grand Canal was reputed to carry around 100,000 passengers a year up to the middle of the 1800s and was used by freight barges up to the 1960s. Once the canal reached Robertstown the development of the village itself began, including the building of the Grand Canal Hotel. The first manager in 1801 was Mr Andrew McMillan. The standard of cuisine and accommodation was considered to be one of the best in its day and due to demand the hotel was extended. However, with the decline in passenger traffic on the canal in the 1850s due mainly to the arrival of the railway, the hotel closed. It later became a police headquarters and a camp for Bord na Mona. On the day we passed, it was for sale.

At Robertstown there are two route options. You can cross Binn's Bridge to the right canal bank and cycle to Lowtown to see the Barrow Line Canal diverge from the Grand. From Lowtown, continue left at Fenton Bridge along the Barrow Line. Eventually you can cross Herberton Bridge back to the left bank. However, over 0.5 km is track that can be muddy in winter. The total distance from Robertstown to Herberton Bridge is about 2.5 km. The alternative route is not to cross Binn's Bridge in Robertstown but stay on the tarred road on the left bank. However, it veers away from the canal for about 1.5 km eventually returning near Herberton Bridge. There is a pub here if you wish to relax and watch the canal world go by.

From Herberton Bridge cycle on 1 km to see the Milltown Feeder Canal branch away from the Barrow Line, and also nearby is the junction of the Barrow Line and Old Barrow Line. It's worse than a railway junction here. Another 0.5 km will take you to Ballyteige Bridge and Castle. This is a mid-15th-century tower and the rebel Silken Thomas is reputed to have sheltered in it. About 2.5 km from Ballyteige the road turns sharply away from the canal and the flora changes. The ground is boggy and covered in gorse. You will also pass through pleasant woodland before eventually coming to a T-junction leading onto a busier road. Turn left and note the Hill of Allen ahead on the right of the road, topped with a tower. The side has been gouged out by quarrying. The hill has been associated with the legendary hero Fionn Mac Cumhaill and the Fianna, a band of warriors that protected the High King. A great battle took place here in 722 AD over an adulterous relationship between the King of Leinster and a daughter of the High King of Ireland. Many were slaughtered in the battle including a bard who continued to recite after he was decapitated. The tower was built in 1859 by a local landlord, Sir Gerald Aylmer, and used as a viewing platform. During the building of the tower a giant skeleton of a man was found and thought to be that of Fionn Mac Cumhaill.

15. Grand Canal System (Kildare)

After about 2.5 km from the T-junction you will come to a cross-roads and junction with the R415. If you feel like it, detour left onto the R415 for Kilmeague 2 km away. On the way you pass through Allen with its fine church whose steeple can be seen from miles around. At Kilmeague another fine, old church dominates the village, established as a refuge for Protestants by the Reverend Preston *c*. 1837. In the village centre turn right taking the road to Naas and admire the pleasant view as you cycle. After 3 km turn left onto the main road. A further 4 km will take you over the railway line going south from Dublin. Soon after is a wooded area, and located here is an old flour mill and water wheel. Nearby the River Liffey passes under the arched Victoria Bridge built in 1837, which you now cross. Cycle on to the first roundabout at the M7, and after crossing over the motorway turn left at the second roundabout for Naas. On the outskirts of town are the considerable ruins of Jigginstown House on your right. This was one of the first brick houses built in the country and was intended for Charles I. It was built by Thomas Wentworth, Earl of Strafford, during the 1630s. Reputedly, he never saw it completed as he was beheaded in 1641, having been charged with treason. Naas itself was a residence of the Leinster kings and is now a busy town with many fine, old buildings. In the town centre is the courthouse built in 1807 and nearby is the town hall refurbished in 1861 from an 18th-century prison.

At the near corner of the town hall turn left followed by right and left again. This will bring you to the Naas branch of the Grand Canal. Turn right, before crossing Abbey Bridge, staying on the right bank of the canal and continue to Tandy's Bridge. Cross the bridge, and turn right following the left bank. The cycle along here is pleasant with trees lining both banks of the canal. About 1 km from Tandy's Bridge, you will pass under the motorway and come to Osberstown Bridge. After this, turn right to pass under the railway bridge and continue to the Leinster Aqueduct. This 5-arched structure, built in 1780, carries the canal and road over the River Liffey, a great engineering feat of the time. Soon after, we saw a grey heron perched on the canal bank. Anxiously, he flew behind us when we stopped to observe him. The next bridge is Digby Bridge dated 1794. A member of the Digby family was a director of the canal company. Turn left here and then right. The canal disappears behind foliage but soon emerges again with trees lining both banks. Continue on, and cross Landenstown Bridge.

15. Grand Canal System (Kildare)

We came across two mute swans, which were less shy than the heron we saw previously. They moved to greet us. A little over 1 km from Landenstown Bridge, the road veers away from the canal towards Prosperous. On the way you pass Killybegs, a demesne once owned by the Brookes family. In 1776 Robert Brooke set up cotton manufacturing in Prosperous. The business venture was never financially successful and it failed within a decade. As you enter the outskirts of the village note the sculpture on the left, near the speed restriction. It is of a bird perched within a stone window. Soon after you will come to the main junction in the centre of the village. Turn left here and back to your car, or if you're peckish treat yourself to a snack in the local café.

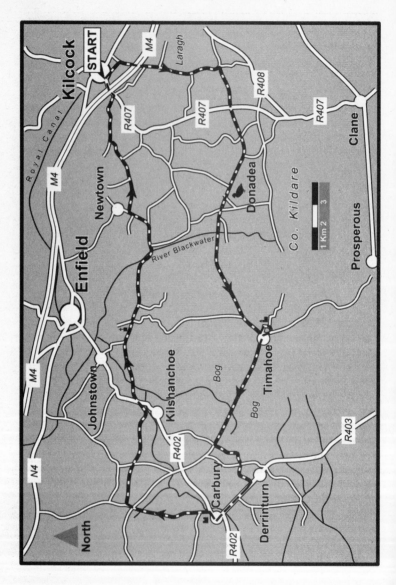

Distance (km)	61
Cycling time (hours)	6
Terrain	Flat
Roads (OSI 49 map)	Mainly third-class
Attractions	Bog, Canal, Wildlife area, Woodland, Heritage

Although rather long, this is an easy cycle as the terrain is flat except for a couple of gentle climbs. The route begins at Kilcock near the Royal Canal and follows through lush Kildare countryside to Donadea. Here there is a pleasant forest park and a lake filled with waterfowl, after which the route continues to Timahoe once used as a camp by the rebels of 1798. It then passes through a bog to Carbury, an ancient place where excavated evidence of the Iron Age has been found. The hill at Carbury is the highest around at 142 m and the views from here are as good as it gets in the area. After Carbury, it is on to Dunfierth where there is an interesting medieval tomb in an old cemetery. After passing Knockanally House and Golf Club the route gently ascends, and then descends to level out again and finish back in Kilcock.

Take the N4/M4 past Maynooth and exit for Kilcock. Follow the signs into town where you should find parking around the town centre and especially the Square. Kilcock is about 34 km from Dublin City.

Once on your bicycle, cross over the canal and railway line towards the Fair Green. Turn immediately left after passing the railway station on your left — the area here is called the Fair Green. Apparently in the 1670s there was a religious dispute in Kilcock. During the row the Archbishop of Dublin banned an itinerant Dominican friar by the name of John Byrne from celebrating religious services. The order was read publicly by the local parish priest to a large gathering around the Fair Green in 1672. However, the poor friar ignored the order, was excommunicated, and landed himself in jail.

After the railway station, the road runs for about 1 km along the railway line and then takes a sharp right away from it. Continue for another 1 km and cross over the M4 motorway. After 1 km the road bends sharply to the left, turn immediately right after the bend. Another 3 km will take you to a crossroads, turn right at the yield sign for Donadea, about 5 km from here. Continue on to a stop sign and cross the R407. Later at another stop sign turn right following the direction of a rusty sign for Knockanally Golf Club. Another 1.5 km will bring you to the entrance of Donadea Forest Park, turn left into it.

Donadea Demesne has been traced to 1312 when Sir Walter Fitzhenry owned it. Eventually it was granted to the Aylmers *c.* 1597, and remained within the family until the 1930s when it was taken over by the State. Unfortunately the Castle has been allowed to decline since. Originally built by Sir Gerald Aylmer *c.* 1624, it was damaged in 1641, rebuilt in 1773, and more recently redesigned by the architect Sir Richard Morrison in 1827. During the mid-1800s the estate itself was extensively developed resulting in the forests and artificial lake there today. The lake provides a habitat for swans and ducks and for coarse fish like rudd and perch. Amongst young oak and ash trees is a memorial to the victims of 9/11. The memorial was inspired by Sean Tallon, a local man, who lost his life as a firefighter attempting to rescue those in the North Tower in New York.

Exit the Demesne from St Peter's Church through a set of gates that lead to the castellated entrance on the main road. Then turn left in the direction of Timahoe about 8 km away. Cycle across Ballagh Crossroads, 1 km from Donadea. There is an old pub here, established in 1812, called Connolly's. After 5 km is another junction, go straight ahead and take the first left about 1 km further on. A couple of hundred metres on the left is an old cemetery with a commemorative plaque to the volunteers of 1798. The main rebel army in the north of Kildare camped around the bogs of Timahoe. They were led by William Aylmer and attacked Kilcock in early June, burning the barracks and courthouse and routing the yeomanry under Sir Fenton Aylmer. General Champagne attacked and dispersed the camp at Timahoe about a week later. However, the rebels regrouped and continued their doomed campaign. Finally on 21 July, William Aylmer surrendered and the camp at Timahoe disbanded.

Continue on to a T-junction and turn right, followed soon by another right at a pub, and at the next junction go left. The circuit from the cemetery to here is less than 1 km. Soon you pass through a wooded area, followed by open boggy ground. About 3 km from Timahoe you cross over a narrow-gauge railway line leading into the bog. Soon after is a petite and pretty thatched cottage on the right.

Turn left for Derrinturn at a crossroads 3 km from the railway. Derrinturn is another 3 km. Close to the village is a stop sign, turn left, and in the village turn right onto the R403 in the direction of Carbury, 2.5 km away. As you cycle into Carbury you will see the belfry of the Church of Ireland church. Head for this and you will be taken to Carbury Hill, also known as Fairy Hill. There is evidence of occupation here dating back to 300 BC. The ruins at the side of the hill are of a great Tudor mansion built by the Colleys. Through marriage the Colleys took the name Wellesley, and their most celebrated member was the Duke of Wellington.

Return to the main road and continue a little, taking the first left and following the sign for the Kildare Tourist Route. At the next junction continue straight on, passing over a bog-railway line. Another 3 km will bring you to a yield sign, turn right in the direction of Broadford, and take another right about 0.5 km away. After 2 km is a crossroads, cycle straight ahead. Kilshanchoe is about 3 km further and you will arrive at a junction on the outskirts of the village. Turn left followed by right. The route now passes by a plethora of modern bungalows separated by fields of grazing sheep. After 2.5 km you come to a stop sign, turn right for about 1 km to a crossroads. On the left in a cemetery are the ruins of Dunfierth Church. This medieval church contains a mortuary chapel enclosing the effigy and tomb of Sir Walter Bermingham who died in 1548. The effigy shows the knight, holding a sword, with his feet resting on a lion. The sides of the chapel contain carvings of 12 saints, 6 on each side, and the back wall depicts the Crucifixion.

Return to the main road and continue for about 4 km where you will pass over the River Blackwater and arrive at a junction by Knockanally Golf Club. At the stop sign go straight on. The road begins to ascend through rather pleasant foliage filled with tuneful birdsong (in June anyway). Take the second turn to the right, the one on the descent. Make sure you do not speed past it, or else you will end in Newtown. After you take the right turn, the village of Newtown will be to your left. The modern houses are in stark contrast to the old church belfry in the middle of them. Follow the road for about 6 km to a stop sign, and then turn left for Kilcock, 1 km away. Cross over the M4 and turn left off the roundabout into town. Finally cross the railway and canal back into town, and to your car. By the way Kilcock is named after St Coca, an embroiderer of church vestments.

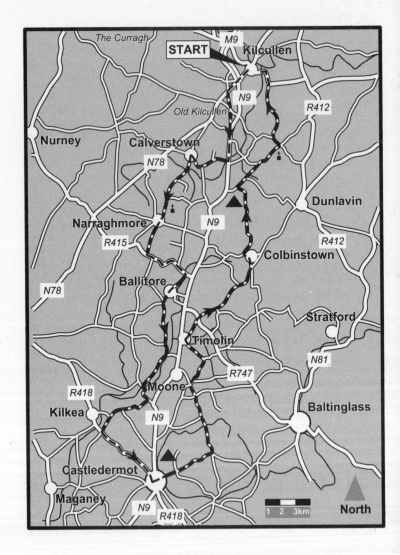

Distance (km)	74
Cycling time (hours)	$7^1/_4$
Terrain	Rolling
Roads (OSI 55, 61 maps)	Third-class roads, except for about 4 km on regional and 3 km on national
Attractions	Rivers, Woodland, Scenic hills, Heritage

This part of Kildare is quite hilly, being near Wicklow I suppose. The route is a long one and together with the rolling countryside makes it quite challenging, particularly on the way back. However, it is a lovely cycle, visiting a number of important heritage sites along the way. The route starts at Kilcullen on the River Liffey and heads for the ancient tower and holy crosses at Old Kilcullen nearby. It continues through the villages of Calverstown and Narraghmore before eventually coming to the ancient abbey and 7th-century High Cross at Moone. Halfway, at Castledermot, is the only hog-backed Viking gravestone in the country. The route returns on rustic roads that meander up and down rolling hills, passing by Timolin and a pewter factory located there. Finishing back at Kilcullen, you can relax in one of the local hostelries and enjoy that tired but very satisfying feeling after a good day's work.

From the City take the N7/M7 past Naas and then exit onto the M9 towards Carlow. After 7 km exit the M9 at the sign for Kilcullen, and follow the signs to the town, about 48 km from Dublin. Probably the best place to find parking is near the Liffey, so drive through the town and over the bridge. You should find parking around here.

Cycle back up through the town towards the M9. Pass over the motorway on the N78 towards Athy. About 1 km from the motorway turn left at the staggered crossroads onto a third-class road. Pass the memorial in Irish to the 1798 Rebellion on the right-hand side. In less that 1 km you will come to the Old Kilcullen graveyard on the left. This is the site of an early monastery whose abbot McTail was ordained by St Patrick. The truncated round tower probably dates from the 11th century and like others around the country was used for protection from Viking raids. There are also the remains of three sculptured high crosses, evidence of the monastic settlement. Looking northwest from the graveyard you should see the hill at Knockaulin upon which was Dun Ailinne, an ancient fort. This is reputed to have been a royal residence of the Kings of Leinster. East of the graveyard are the Wicklow Mountains.

The road descends for about 1 km to the busy N9, turn right onto it. After 2 km turn right at the staggered crossroads for Calverstown, 3 km further. At the crossroads at Calverstown turn left in the direction of Narraghmore. On the outskirts of Narraghmore you will come to a yield sign, turn right into the village. Then take the first turn to the left before the village square. About 1 km from the village is the Church of the Holy Saviour, off the road on the left. St Patrick may have founded a church on this site. Past the church the road becomes lined with broad-leaved trees before coming to a junction with the R415. Turn left and the road descends towards Ballitore with distant views of the Wicklow Mountains ahead. After 2.5 km fork right at the sign for Ballitore. Cycle another 2 km to the next crossroads and turn left. Here there is a quaint, slated cottage facing you. This is a quiet, pleasant road upon which I saw a number of rabbits foraging alongside. They scurried into the ditch on my approach. Apparently a bolting rabbit exposes the white underside of its tail as a signal to other rabbits of danger. Watch for the sign for Moone High Cross and Abbey about 3 km from the cottage. Moone High Cross is an important monument dating back to the 7th century. The 5-m-high granite structure is sculptured with scenes from the Old and New Testaments, and reckoned to be the masterpiece amongst other high crosses nearby, at Old Kilcullen and Castledermot. The medieval friary also here dates from around 1300 and probably built by the Franciscans. It was dissolved by the English King Henry VIII around 1540.

Continue after leaving Moone High Cross and Abbey to the next right-turn nearby. It's worth continuing a little past the turn to Moone Bridge, over the River Greese. The scene here is very pleasant with the river flowing through mature foliage which partly conceals a ruined 18th-century mansion, owned by the Yeates family. Return to the turn, now to your left, and take it. Initially this tree-lined road follows the river for about 0.5 km. Then the river veers away and the trees give way to more open ground. The road terminates at a T-junction about 2 km on. At the junction is the ruins of a multi-sided building. Turn left and after passing through a series of bad turns turn right, following the sign for Kilkea Castle and Golf Club. On the day I passed, the pungent aroma of newly-mown grass was particularly pleasant to my senses. After 4 km you will pass the entrance to Kilkea Castle and Golf Club, and at the Y-junction just after keep left. Soon you come to the R418. Turn left again for Castledermot, about 4.5 km away. The road rises to Mullaghreelan Forest on the left, planted with conifers as well as oak, beech, birch, ash and sycamore. This is a picnic area with walking paths. Near the entrance is an inscribed stone to the memory of Laurence O'Toole, 12th-century Abbot of Glendalough and Archbishop of Dublin. Born nearby here, he was the first Irish saint to be canonised by Rome. Continue on to Castledermot where the R418 meets the N9. Turn right onto the N9 and then first left at the sign for the High Cross and Round Tower.

The town of Castledermot can trace its roots to the 9th century when the hermit St Diarmada, a grandson of an Ulster king, resided by the River Graney. A monastic settlement developed, as evidenced by the castellated round tower, high crosses and reconstructed Romanesque portal. The Norsemen raided this place a number of times and there is a hog-back Viking grave-marker. This is decorated with crosses and lozenges and represents a long house, typical of a Norse dwelling. Return to the N9 and continue a little further up town to the remains of a Franciscan friary on the right. This fine structure originates from *c.* 1247. In 1317 a Scottish army under Edward Bruce destroyed the friary when he tried to take the town. However, it was rebuilt soon after and extended.

Head back up the town and take the first right past the pedestrian traffic lights. This is opposite the R418, the road you came in on. As you cycle, note on the left a lonely hill topped with trees called Narraghbeg. Continue to the second set of crossroads about 4 km from Castledermot. Here you will find the remains of a blacksmith shop. Turn left and climb a steep hill for about 1 km before descending. Another 3 km will take you to another crossroads. Continue straight through for less than 1 km to a T-junction and turn right. At the next crossroads nearby continue straight on. There is an old church and cemetery on the left at these crossroads. Follow the road for about 3 km to Timolin keeping left at a Y-junction. As you enter Timolin look for the pewter factory on the right-hand side located in an old mill. Pewter, like bronze, is the oldest of alloys. Warriors of the Bronze

Age would celebrate their victories by drinking from pewter vessels. Today the old tradition of pewter quality is maintained at Timolin, and the pewter here is reputed to be of the highest finish.

After the factory continue to the stop sign in the centre of the village and turn right. Soon after you come to a Y-junction, turn right. There is a steady climb from Timolin for about 1 km. About 1 km from the Y-junction is a stop sign at the R747. Cycle straight across in the direction of the sign for Rathsallagh. This road runs on the Kildare/Wicklow border for about 2 km. After 3.5 km from the R747 you pass the Church of the Ascension at Ballynure on the left. Another 1 km will take you to a crossroads after descending a hill. Turn left in the direction of Kilcullen, then take the second turn on the right about 1 km further just after crossing the River Greese. After 1 km, you come to a site with standing stones and newly-planted trees. The road now rises to 190 m above sea level near Brewel Hill before descending steeply to a T-junction. Turn right. Cycle on for about 3.5 km to Gormanstown Crossroads marked by a church. Turn left here at the stop sign in the direction of Kilcullen. Keep right at the Y-junction about 1 km further on, staying on the main road. The road now begins to descend passing Gilltown Stud on the right-hand side. After 1 km the road joins the R413 that takes you into Kilcullen to a set of traffic lights. Turn right here to return to your car. Kilcullen has a number of establishments for you to take a well-deserved treat and rest, if you so fancy.

18. Barrow Line (Kildare, Laois)

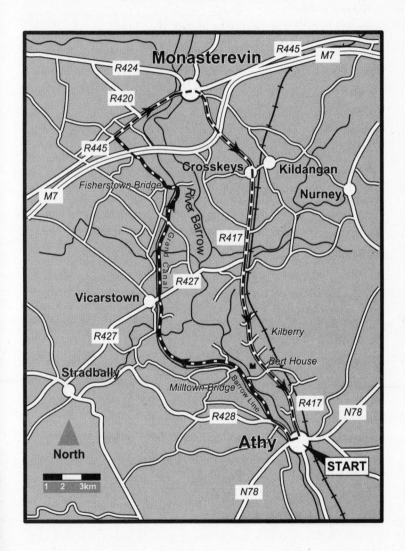

18. Barrow Line (Kildare, Laois)

Distance (km)	47
Cycling time (hours)	$3^1/4$
Terrain	Flat
Roads (OSI 55 map)	About half on regional, the remainder on third-class except for 1.5 km on track and 4 km on the N7
Attractions	Canal, River, some Woodland, Heritage

This is an easy cycle that includes a section of the Barrow Line. The Barrow Line is part of the Grand Canal system, and connects the River Barrow at Athy to the Grand Canal at Robertstown. It was completed c. 1791. The cycle starts from the heritage town of Athy and follows the canal to the old industrial centre of Monasterevin; there is a small section of the route on grass track. The countryside here is flat and rather plain but there are interesting features along the canal and the mood is one of rural serenity. The atmosphere must have been very different when the canal was being constructed — you could imagine the clamour of men and machines forging the duct. Away from the canal, the return route passes by Moore Abbey Forest Park with its mix of conifers and broad-leaf trees. It continues through the villages of Kildangan, and Kilberry with the imposing Bert House nearby, before finishing back in Athy.

Take the N7/M7 from the City and exit onto the M9. From the M9, take the N78 to Athy, about 70 km from the City. Continue through Athy to the third bridge. This is the one crossing the canal. Just over the bridge there is a car park to your right, opposite the Bridge House Pub. Park your car here.

Once on your bicycle go left from the car park back over the canal bridge. Take the second left onto the R428 in the direction of Stradbally. Just before the R428 crosses the canal at Cardington Bridge, fork right onto a third-class road. The canal will be to your left, although when we were there it was drained for about 3 km from Cardington Bridge to the next bridge, Milltown Bridge — it looked like dredging was in progress. Between the two bridges the canal is partly hidden by foliage and at one stage the Barrow River meanders quite close, the road being between them. The canal is navigable and as if to refute this we saw a sunken boat. There was quite a lot of reed in the water and I wondered how this would affect a revolving propeller. Sedges and cattail, also called bulrush, are prevalent. Some of these plants are important to the eco system. Cattail, recognised by its dark, soft, sausage-like bit, helps to treat water naturally and also provides shelter for fish and birds.

The canal turning from west to north about 3 km from Milltown Bridge marks the border with County Laois. We knew we had crossed when we saw the blue and white flag of Laois dangling at a local farm. Two grey herons, conspicuous for their broad M-shaped wings and dangling, trailing legs, flew overhead as if to mark the occasion. An unusual animal for these parts is wild mink. They roam the area after many were freed from a nearby mink farm some years ago. Locals are concerned at the damage they do to fish stocks and bird-life. Soon after you will cross over the Stradbally River on an aqueduct, an amazing piece of engineering when you think about it, water on water. Another 1.5 km further brings you to the rural serenity of Vicarstown. Barges and an assortment of other boats were tied to both banks of the canal; some of them were sunk. There are a couple of pubs here if you need to refresh.

The next section, Vicarstown to Monasterevin, is about 12 km long, 4.5 km of which can be demanding cycling, especially after a lot of rain. There are two soft tracks. The first, before Fisherstown Bridge, is about 1.5 km. The second, after the bridge, is about 3 km and scored with deep tractor ruts. About 1.5 km after Vicarstown we met the first track. It had been raining and so was very muddy, but we managed to cycle most of it although slipping quite a lot. We traversed two more aqueducts before reaching Fisherstown Bridge. Amazingly on this section we found an articulated truck on its side. What the truck was doing here I don't know. But the driver must have misjudged the width of the narrow road and toppled over the bank into the adjacent field. It could have just as easily toppled into the canal.

I would advise leaving the canal at Fisherstown Bridge to avoid the second deeply-rutted track. However, if you fancy a challenge you could continue, eventually crossing a timber-decked bridge to a tarred road, and cycling on to meet the N7 where you turn right for Monasterevin. To avoid this track cross Fisherstown Bridge to a quaint thatched pub. Turn right at the pub and cycle directly to the N7. Turn right again at the junction for Monasterevin, altogether about 7 km from Fisherstown Bridge.

Monasterevin gets its name from Saint Evin who founded a monastery here around the 6th century AD. The town prospered and in the 19th century became industrious with a brewery and distillery. One old Georgian building on your way is called the 'Hulk'. This building housed a number of experiments in childcare around the turn of the 18th century. It was eventually closed because of the dreadful conditions. Cycle through Monasterevin to the junction of the Athy road, the R417. At this junction is the entrance to the old Cistercian monastery, Moore Abbey. More recently it was the home of the famous tenor John McCormack but is now occupied by the Sisters of Charity. Turn right onto the R417 and a slight incline will take you to Moore Abbey Forest Park, popular locally for walks. The small hill here is really the only climb on the whole trip.

Continue on for about 3 km to Kildangan. A small detour to the left will take you to the quaint parish church. Notice as you cross the railway line on the way to the church how straight the track runs, characteristic of the flat plains of Kildare. Back on the R417 the road to Kilberry is also straight and partly surrounded by marsh. Clumps of sedge and marsh plants in the sodden ground are in contrast to the richer farming land in the county. A pub marks the halfway stage to Athy. Strangely as we passed we saw no name on it. Shortly after, a small river runs parallel with the road. We met a lone mute swan, recognised from other swan species by its nose knob. This swan is not really mute because it will hiss and snort aggressively when annoyed.

In Kilberry there is a fine old church on your right and as you leave the village look for Bert House, off the road to your right. William Burgh built this fine place in the early 18th century. He was a supporter of William of Orange (tours 22, 27) and for his services was rewarded with high official office. In more recent times, the house is associated with a rags-to-riches story. Kildare woman Sheila Connolly emigrated to America in the 1940s and eventually became a model for Ponds. She later entered the movie business and married Harry Danzinger, a Hollywood producer and war hero. He bought her Bert House, an astonishing accomplishment for her; as a young girl she used to cycle past it on her way to school and dream of becoming a kitchen maid there. The house is now a hotel.

18. Barrow Line (Kildare, Laois)

Continue to Athy, 5 km away. The town gets its name from a king of Munster called Ae who was killed here in the 11th century. Athy originated to command an important ford across the River Barrow. As you enter the outskirts of the town the river is to your right and eventually flows under an arched 18th-century bridge, still carrying traffic across town. Across the river to your right are the remains of an old castle called Woodstock. Built by the Anglo-Normans, it was damaged during the Stuart and Jacobite Wars. Soon you will come to traffic lights; facing you is the old market house, now the tourist office, museum and library. Turn right to see the 16th-century White Castle at the river bridge. Once it protected the bridge, now it is a private residence. Continue until you cross the canal bridge and back to your car.

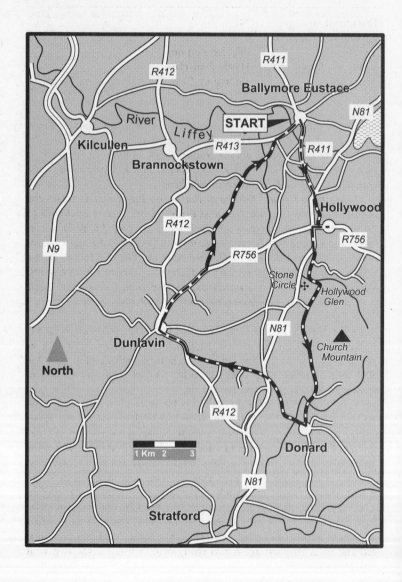

Distance (km)	34
Cycling time (hours)	4
Terrain	Hilly (verging on)
Roads (osi 55, 56 maps)	Mostly third-class
Attractions	Mountains, Glen, Forest, River, some Heritage

This route passes through Hollywood Glen where, it is said, St Kevin had his first hermitage. Although the area is partly mountainous the cycling is not too taxing and just about verges on hilly. The route itself meanders through some delightful villages which have inherited the tranquillity that St Kevin once sought here.

It begins in County Kildare at Ballymore Eustace and crosses the River Liffey over the fine 6-arched bridge there. It then continues to the village of Hollywood — although more associated with St Kevin, it has some tradition of movie-making too. Onwards the route passes through Hollywood Glen to Donard near the Glen of Imaal. In the village centre is an ogham stone, depicting an ancient form of script. After, the route continues northwest to Dunlavin, where Dean Swift once administered, before heading back to Ballymore Eustace.

Take the N81 from the City, or exit 11 off the M50 for the N81. Follow the signs for Blessington. Pass through the town continuing on the N81 for about 5 km, after which turn right at the sign for Ballymore Eustace. The town is about 35 km from the City. You should find parking around the centre.

From the village take the R411 to Hollywood, 6 km away. This will take you over the fine, old, 6-arched bridge crossing the River Liffey. After 1 km you will see a body of water on the left. This is Golden Falls Reservoir, part of a local hydro power station. Watch for an ancient stone circle on the right-hand side just before a crossroads, about 2.5 km from Ballymore Eustace. One legend has it that the granite boulders are dancers who were turned to stone for dancing on a Sunday. More likely it was arranged as a pre-Christian religious site. Less than 1 km later is a junction with the N81. Cycle straight across and on to another junction with the R756, about 1.5 km away. Turn left and soon after left again into Hollywood. Closely associated with

19. Hollywood Glen (Kildare, Wicklow)

St Kevin, it was said that the village got its name from a wood that blocked St Kevin's path to Glendalough. Miraculously the wood flattened, forming a path for the saint. But once he passed, the trees rose again blocking anyone wanting to follow, thus the name 'Holy Wood'. Like its Californian namesake, Hollywood also has a movie tradition. Brian Friel's 'Dancing at Lughnasa', starring Meryl Streep, was made here. The day we visited, a commercial for Budweiser was being filmed. The theme seemed to be about a Wicklow rodeo, imagine that!

Return to the R756 and turn right. Continue to the busy N81 nearby and turn left. You will not have to stay on this busy road, because in less than 1 km there is a turn to the left, at a sign for Athgreany. Take this turn to bring you through Hollywood Glen. Overshadowed by Church Mountain on the east side, it is an area of trees, peace and tranquillity. It is easy to understand why St Kevin might have had his first hermitage here. The Glen runs for about 2 km, after which another 3 km should take you to Donard. On the way in to the village you will pass churches right and left before coming to a crossroads at the post office. Cycle straight on to the centre of the village. This is a pretty place, and in the centre is an ogham stone near the statue of the Virgin. Ogham is a form of alphabet originating from the Celts. It is thought to have been used primarily on grave and boundary markers and examples have been found on standing stones such as the one here. Basically ogham letters consist of combinations of perpendicular or angled strokes, meeting or crossing a centre line. However, the Donard stone seems the worse for wear and it is difficult to make out much.

Return to the crossroads at the post office and turn left. There is an incline as you cycle away from Clonard. After the climb you will descend to the N81 at a junction and pub, about 3 km from Donard. Cycle straight across following the sign for Boherboy. After 2 km the road begins to ascend again for about 1 km, and then falls to a junction with the R412. At the yield sign turn right for Dunlavin, about 1 km away. The town of Dunlavin is conspicuous for its broad main street, before which is a memorial, near the RC church, to those who were massacred here in 1798. Thirty-six men, suspected members of the United Irishmen, were taken to this green and shot without warning by a Wicklow regiment; only one man survived by faking his death. The commander had panicked, fearing an attack on the garrison, and shot the men as a deterrent. Needless to say the action left terrible memories in the village for years to come. At the top of the main street turn right, staying on the R412. Ahead is the fine old courthouse. Built in the Doric style of Grecian architecture in the late 1700s, it is attributed to a local landlord by the name of Tynte.

Cycle on to a nearby Y-junction where you turn right onto the R756. This is in the direction of Ballymore Eustace, about 11 km away. After 2 km you will pass Tober Demesne on the left and the ruin of old house. Another 1 km should take you to a Y-junction. Fork left off the R756 following the sign for Ballymore Eustace. Continue cycling to within 1 km of the town where there is a junction onto the R413, turn right here. Continue to a stop sign with the R411, turn left and over the Liffey into the town centre. Ballymore Eustace gets its name from the Anglo-Norman Thomas FitzEustace who was appointed a constable here. A fort was built to protect the river-crossing from marauding native Irish. They had been forced into the mountains by the Anglo-Normans and were not at all a happy lot. Thankfully since then, times have changed and today you can enjoy the native hospitality without fear of attack.

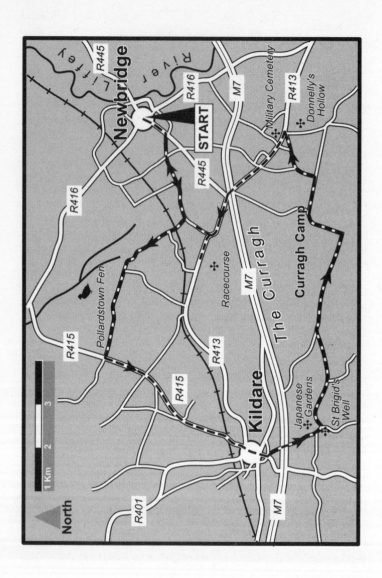

Distance (km)	35
Cycling time (hours)	4¹/₄
Terrain	Flat
Roads (osi 55 map)	Third-class except for about 6 km on regional
Attractions	Curragh plain, Gardens, Wildlife sanctuary, Equestrian centres, Heritage

This circuit around the Curragh is a lovely one and the Curragh's equestrian tradition is everywhere. The route is flat and easy with contrasting landscape and plenty to see. It starts at Newbridge and heads for the wildlife of Pollardstown Fen, an important nature reserve. It then continues to the ancient town of Kildare with its fine medieval cathedral. Near by, you can rest at St Brigid's Well and enjoy the tranquil mood, or visit the magnificent Japanese Gardens, depicting man's progress through life. Then it is on to the Curragh Military camp, itself a historic place surrounded by the landscape that has made this county famous. It is also the site of a great and well-attended boxing contest held in the early 19th century. The route finishes back in the busy town of Newbridge, but not without detouring to see the home of the Irish Derby, the Curragh Racecourse.

Take the N7/M7 and exit at the sign for Newbridge. Follow the signs to the town, about 43 km from the City. Drive through Newbridge until you see a Ford garage on your right. Turn right at the garage and veer left. Continue a short distance to an old church, St Patrick's Church of Ireland. Park your car around here.

Keeping right of the church, cycle on through a set of traffic lights and past the housing estates. Once in open country take a right turn at a sign for Pollardstown Fen about 1.5 km from St Patrick's Church. Shortly after you will pass over the railway and at the following junction keep right. After another 1.5 km you will come to another junction, keep going straight. On the day we were here the sign for Pollardstown Fen was pointing in the wrong direction. Another 1 km will bring you to the gate of the Fen on the right, on a bend. It is easy to miss — if you come to a cemetery and church ruin on your right, you have passed it. Pollardstown Fen, developed after the last Ice Age, is an alkaline marsh fed by springs from the Curragh Plain. It is a rare habitat and home to a number of rare flora and fauna; this makes it an internationally important site. The vegetation hides many of its residents such as the elusive otter and Ireland's smallest duck, the teal.

Continue for about 2 km until you come to the junction with the R415. Turn left for one of the oldest towns in Ireland, around 4 km away. As you enter Kildare you will see its ancient round tower, with a more modern battlemented top, and St Brigid's Cathedral on the right. Kildare or *Cill Dara* means the church of the oak and is associated with St Brigid. Her feast day, 1 February, traditionally heralds the beginning of spring. She is said to have founded a monastery here beside an oak tree. The site was also a shrine for the Celtic druids. This has posed the question whether St Brigid was a historic personage or a derivation of the Celtic pagan goddess Brigid. Anyway the monastery itself flourished from the 6th century until the Norsemen arrived and sacked the town. Later St Brigid's Cathedral, an early example of Gothic architecture, was built on the site of the monastery by the Normans *c.* 1223. It was destroyed in the 17th century but restored again in the 19th. The grounds contain interesting remnants of the site's long history — a round tower, a Celtic cross and St Brigid's Firehouse. It is open to visitors from May to October and the entrance is near the tourist office, located in the town centre.

From the centre of town continue on through the traffic lights on the R415. Veer left onto a third-class road at the signs for the Japanese Gardens, National Stud and St Brigid's Well. After 1 km turn right and then left for St Brigid's Well. The directions are signposted. This is a holy and peaceful place where pilgrims place their votive offerings, pieces of cloth, on the surrounding trees. St Brigid is associated with miracles of healing. Close by are the Japanese Gardens, and the Irish National Stud and Horse Museum where the history of the horse in Ireland can be traced. The Japanese Gardens were created in 1906 by a team of Japanese gardeners employed by the aptly-named Lord Wavertree. The path through the gardens symbolises man's journey from the cradle to the grave. The features are open from February to November and there is an entrance fee.

After the Japanese Gardens, go on to the next junction and veer left at the sign for the Curragh. Another junction will meet you about 1 km further, veer right here towards Kilcullen. You will soon see the military camp ahead of you. As you cycle past Maddenstown the landscape is very open and distinctive of the Curragh. Rich in pasture, as can be seen by the numbers of horses and sheep, the Curragh is a natural store of water and an important irrigation system. It has extensive sand and gravel deposits that hold rainfall and water. The water then contributes to springs that feed the surrounding area. As you approach the military camp you will come to a crossroads. Turn left here at a sign for Newbridge. A 1-km cycle will bring you into the centre of the camp and keep in mind that there may be road restrictions. The British built this camp in 1855 to train soldiers for the Crimean War. It was taken over by the Irish Army in 1922 after the War of Independence. Turn right at the post office and on your left you will see one of the original buildings, the Clock Tower.

Follow the road to exit the camp at the golf club. Turn left at the exit and next right. Soon you will come to a junction with the R413. Just right of this junction is Donnelly's Hollow; left will take you to Newbridge. It was at this natural amphitheatre that crowds gathered to watch the underdog Dan Donnelly defeat the English champion George Cooper. The fight went to 11 rounds with Donnelly finally knocking Cooper out. Unfortunately Donnelly's wiliness in the ring failed him outside, and he died impoverished at the age of 32. His preserved arm used to be on show in the Hideout Pub in Kilcullen, but not anymore — it got the elbow! Nearby on the right, on the way to Newbridge, is the military cemetery. This is a simple place with plain headstones remembering soldiers and their families going back to when the military camp was established.

Continue on towards Newbridge to a roundabout, about 1.5 km away. Follow the signs for Newbridge/Racecourse and go over the motorway to a second roundabout. You can detour here to the Curragh Racecourse about 1 km away. This is the leading racing venue in the country hosting many of the classics, including the Irish Derby which originated in 1866. Although horseracing in the Curragh area is said to have taken place before Christianity, the first races to be run here go back just to the 18th century. In 1745 Padreen Mare won the King's Plate, worth 100 guineas. Apparently the horse got its name because the owner hung rosary beads on her collar; *paidrin* is the Irish for rosary beads. There are many training establishments in the neighbourhood and these along with the Irish National Stud make Kildare the equestrian capital of Ireland.

20. The Curragh of Kildare (Kildare)

Continue your cycle by taking the third-class road opposite the large effigy of the filly, Ridgewood Pearl. At the next junction keep right and cycle back to St Patrick's Church and your car, less than 2 km from the junction.

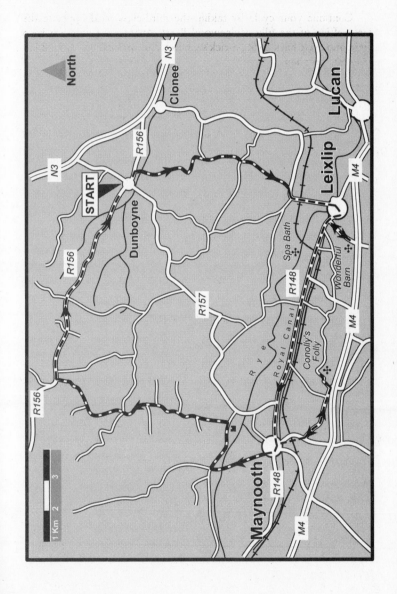

21. Royal Canal (Kildare, Meath)

Distance (km)	38
Cycling time (hours)	$3^3/4$
Terrain	Flat
Roads (osi 50 map)	Half on regional and half on third-class
Attractions	Rivers, Canal, Conservation area, Heritage

In part this cycle passes near the serene Royal Canal, constructed in the late 18th century to provide a transport system between Dublin and the River Shannon. The route begins at Dunboyne and progresses to the old Viking town of Leixlip, where the peculiar Wonderful Barn is located. At Leixlip it meets the Royal Canal, and runs part of the way beside it to Maynooth. This old university town grew around the Anglo-Norman castle there, but is more famous for its long-serving pontifical university. The eccentric Conolly's Folly nearby is worth a detour. The route then turns away from the canal through flat, grazing country, finally completing back in Dunboyne. Overall this is an easy cycle, and the only hill of any test is out of Leixlip on the way to Maynooth.

Take the N3 from the City past Blanchardstown, and then turn off onto the R156 for Clonee/Dunboyne. Follow the signs to Dunboyne, about 19 km from the City. Park your car around the village green near the church.

Cycle back in the direction you came and take the first turn to the right. Although there is no sign for Leixlip here, there is a sign for a cemetery amongst others. Soon after you should hear the coarse call of rooks as you draw near it. Past the cemetery is a junction; continue straight for Leixlip, 5 km away. After another 1 km you approach a stop sign at a crossroads. Go straight across for another 2 km to the R149. Turn right, and soon after left, following the sign for Leixlip. Cross Cope Bridge over the Royal Canal and railway line. There are traffic lights controlling access to this narrow bridge. Continue until you eventually descend Captain's Hill into the town. Turn right at the traffic lights at the bottom. Within a short distance and on the left is the town-centre car park, turn in here. Look for the tourist information board. Leixlip was founded by the Danes in the early 10th century. It gets its name from a salmon leap that was once nearby, and is now replaced by a dam for hydroelectric power. There are a number of interesting sights to be seen from the car park. The waters of the Rivers Liffey and Rye Water meet at an old boathouse. St Mary's Church has a fine medieval tower — Archbishop Price of Cashel is interred here. He bequeathed money to Richard Guinness, father of the famous Arthur who developed a brewery in Leixlip in 1756. Leixlip Castle opposite, behind the trees, was originally built around 1172 by the Anglo-Norman Adam de Hereford. It was a stronghold of the Pale and suffered many assaults during these times and later. It is now privately owned and opened to the public occasionally.

Return to the main street and continue. You will cross a bridge over the Rye Water. This river was once the border of the ancient kingdoms of Leinster and Meath. An area around the river has been designated a Special Area of Conservation, a unique habitat for flora and fauna in an urban environment. Amongst the many insects are the long-bodied dragonflies and damselflies. Species such as the metallic-blue demoiselle damselfly can be seen hovering above the water's surface in summer, a beautiful insect. Continue up the hill and past the church on the left. Detour at the next left for the Wonderful Barn at the sign for Celbridge. Cycle for about 1 km until you pass the built-up areas and soon you will see the top of the Wonderful Barn. There is a turn to the right where you can gain access. This strange structure was built *c*. 1743 and was used to store grain. It has a conical shape and steps on the outside that go all the way to the top. There are two smaller versions beside it — most unusual.

Return to the main route and continue to Louisa Bridge, crossing the canal and railway. Turn immediately right into a sorry-looking car park. If you follow a grass footpath from the car park (not the towpath) you will come to an old stone bath with steps into it. This is a remnant of the old spa that Leixlip was once famous for. People would travel all the way from the city to take advantage of its waters. Return to the main road, the R148, and continue on, in the direction of Maynooth. The canal veers away from the road and after 1.5 km returns running alongside, but it cannot be seen for the trees until you come to Pike Bridge at the Carton House Golf Club. The Royal Canal's 145 kilometres were built around the turn of the 18th century, later than its sister the Grand Canal. But it never attained the same success as the Grand, and the railway saw to its demise as a commercial enterprise. Today both canals are being developed as leisure amenities and natural habitats.

Continue to Maynooth, about 2 km from Pike Bridge. The town of Maynooth probably grew around the Anglo-Norman castle built here by the Fitzgeralds. The family crest includes a monkey said to have saved the First Earl of Kildare from a fire when he was a baby. Centuries later, during the rebellion of Silken Thomas, the foster brother of Silken Thomas betrayed the castle to the English forces. The English paid a reward to the traitor, and then promptly chopped his head off, or said more eloquently at the time, 'caused him to be cut shorter by a head'. To see a piece of eccentric local history, take a detour to Conolly's Folly, a 6-km round trip. Turn left in the town centre at traffic lights for Clane/Celbridge. Soon after, at the Maxol garage, turn left for Celbridge and pass the built-up areas. Eventually the top of the monument will come into view. Take the left at a cluster of bungalows and Conolly's Folly is a few hundred metres further on the right. This 45-m structure was designed by Richard Castle, and built by the Conollys of Castletown near Celbridge *c*. 1739 to give employment during a famine. It consists of 5 varied arches upon which is mounted an obelisk — a fine folly, you could say.

Return to the centre of Maynooth and turn left at the traffic lights to the university. The Anglo-Norman castle is also here, and St Mary's Church, a place of worship for 800 years. The university goes back to 1795, and founded for the training of priests because the government feared the influence of revolutionary ideas at continental colleges. More recently in 1966 it was opened to lay students. From the university, head back towards the town centre, but turn left towards Kilcock on the R148. At the church, fork right onto a third-class road. Continue for about 2 km and cross the Rye Water, marking the Kildare/Meath border, to a staggered crossroads. Turn right and just before the ruin of an old castle turn left. The surrounding country contains grazing land as evidenced by the many horses. Of course Meath, like Kildare, has an illustrious equestrian tradition. The greatest steeplechaser ever, Arkle, was foaled at Ballymacoll Stud near Dunboyne. Pass through Kilcloon, eventually coming to the junction with the R156. The distance from the ruined castle to here is about 5 km. Turn right for Dunboyne, about 7 km away, and back to your car.

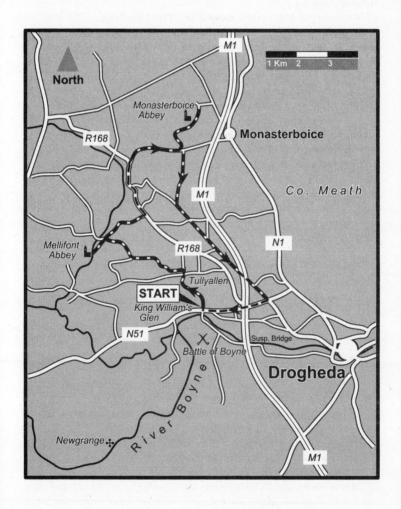

Distance (km)	26
Cycling time (hours)	3
Terrain	Hilly
Roads (osi 36, 43 maps)	Half on regional, the remainder on third-class except for 2 km on busy N51
Attractions	River, Scenic hills, Heritage

Here is an opportunity to visit two ancient abbeys spanning 1,000 years. The abbeys of Mellifont and Monasterboice were significant centres of ecclesiastical and learning excellence. The learned men who founded these monasteries selected sites that would assert their import-ance. They are therefore located on high ground, and unfortunately the abbots did not take the cyclist into consideration. Hence this is a hilly route but well rewarded for its heritage and scenery. I have included some alternatives for those wishing to avoid the more robust climbs. The route begins west of Drogheda on the north bank of the River Boyne. It gently climbs through the delightful King William's Glen to Tullyallen and then to the 12th-century Mellifont Abbey. It continues to the 6th-century Monasterboice site close by. The return route presents fine views of a possible future historic monument, the far more recent M1 suspension bridge over the River Boyne.

The most convenient way to get to the start of this route is to take the M1 motorway to Drogheda. You will need to pay a bridge toll near Drogheda. After passing the tollbooth and crossing the suspension bridge, exit for the N51/Slane. Once on the N51 the Boyne will emerge to your left. After passing signs for the Battle of the Boyne look out for the car parks left and right of the road. You can park here.

Cycle back to the Battle of the Boyne signs and turn left. There is a 1.5-km hill climb through the pleasant setting of King William's Glen, midst the sounds of a gushing stream. As I pushed on the pedals I wondered what this Dutch king was like, he who had left Ireland a legacy so pertinent today. William of Orange was born in 1650 just 8 days after the death of his father. He suffered from asthma and grew up to be a small man, slightly stooped with a beaked nose. As a Calvinist he preferred to dress soberly and speak plainly and honestly.

Many regarded him as a cold and stern person, without tact. He married the daughter of the man he would fight at the Boyne, James II. William's plain speaking and looks did not go down well with his new 15-year-old bride, Mary, or the foppish English court he was about to rule. But she came to admire his dogged determination and eventually adopted his faith. His character showed at the Boyne where he led from the front, even after being wounded at an earlier reconnaissance. William died in 1702 from complications after falling from his horse. His death brought to an end the Dutch House of Orange but paved the way for the future Orange Order.

From King William's Glen, you will emerge at a crossroads at Tullyallen with a school to your right. Cross towards the school. You can choose to take the shorter, hillier route with great views by turning left just past the school, and following the road for about 3 km to a crossroads. Turn left for Mellifont, which is close by. For an easier and longer alternative (4 km), continue past the school to the R168 and turn left. Follow the signs to Mellifont. I was the only visitor on the day I was here. I found it very peaceful listening to the lively chirruping of a skylark and the gentle flow of the nearby River Mattock. Mellifont was the first Cistercian abbey in Ireland, founded by St Malachy O'Morgair. He was strongly influenced by the Cistercian way of life in Clairvaux, France. Upon returning to Ireland he selected the current site for a monastery and the church was consecrated c. 1157. It was a state event attended by the great religious and royal dignitaries of the time. The abbey prospered and by 1170 was said to have 100 monks and 300 lay brothers. However, Henry VIII dissolved it in 1539 in his attempt to curb the power of the Catholic Church. Its history continued to the early 1700s when it was allowed to deteriorate. Unfortunately much of the structure has disappeared. Tours are offered from May to September; however, access to the site is available all year round.

On leaving Mellifont cycle straight on to the R168 and follow the signs to Monasterboice, about 6 km away from Mellifont. As you approach this site you will see the round tower devoid of its top. It was damaged by fire in 1097 along with its books and treasures. St Buite founded the original monastery in the 6th century. It continued to flourish until around 1150. Then its function moved to Mellifont through the church reforms introduced by St Malachy. The main attractions are three crosses dating back to the 10th century. The most important is probably Muiredach's Cross depicting biblical scenes from the Old and New Testaments. Note the scene on the east face illustrating the last judgment where St Michael is weighing a good soul and the devil is pulling the scales from below — a fantastic image? The site is also a cemetery with graves that are both ancient and new. A more recent son of Louth and former Defence Minister, P. S. Donegan, is buried here.

On leaving the site turn right and after 1 km go left. You can choose a shorter, hillier (139 m) and more scenic route by taking the next right. This is a challenging climb to the Hill of Rath. After, it is downhill where you eventually come to a roundabout. Follow the signs for the N51/Slane to a second roundabout. At the second roundabout there is a fine view of the suspension bridge over the River Boyne. The structure was designed to preserve the environment around the river. Cable staying permitted a longer bridge span without the need for supports in the riverbed. The designers also planned to make the bridge appealing. The tall pylon on the south bank together with cable stays fanning to the main structure were the solution. I thought it looked okay; see what you think? From this roundabout follow the signs for the N51/Slane back to your car. Soon the River Boyne will be on your left, flowing against you.

For a less hilly but longer alternative route, turn right on leaving Monasterboice and after 1 km turn left. Cycle to the busy N1 and turn right for Drogheda, about 8 km. In Drogheda take the N51/Slane back to your car.

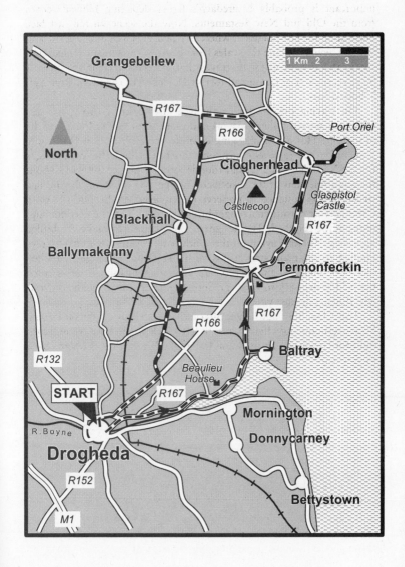

107

Distance (km)	36
Cycling time (hours)	$3^1/2$
Terrain	Rolling
Roads (OSI 36, 43 maps)	Two-thirds on regional, the remainder on third-class
Attractions	Coast, River, Bird-watching, Heritage

This is a pleasant cycle with a number of fascinating places to visit. The first part of the route is quite flat except at Port Oriel; the return, however, is a bit hillier. It begins at Drogheda and follows the north bank of the Boyne downstream where an assortment of waterfowl scuttle across the glistening mudflats at low tide. Further on near Baltray are standing stones linked to the winter solstice. The route continues to Termonfeckin, St Feckin's sacred place, and then along the coast to Clogherhead and the harbour of Port Oriel, popular for sea angling and views of the Mourne Mountains. It returns inland across rolling countryside dotted with the odd charming, little church and shaded road. Cycling through the last remaining gate of Drogheda's once-great medieval wall just about marks the completion of the tour.

You can take the M1 all the way to Drogheda. However, I suggest you come off before the tollbooth. This will save you the toll charge, and take you into the town centre as well. Parking fees are obligatory around the town centre; you can avoid these too. Take the M1 north past Balbriggan and exit for the R132 and Drogheda South. Follow the signs for Julianstown and continue through the village to Drogheda, about 50 km from the City. Near the town centre at St Mary's Church turn right and cross St Mary's Bridge over the River Boyne. Then turn right along the docks. Take the second left at a sign for Baltray followed by an immediate right. Continue on the R167 under the railway viaduct and you should find a suitable place to park by the roadside, about 1.5 km from the town centre.

Once on your bicycle, cycle on towards Baltray with the river on your right. At low tide you can stop and watch the waterfowl feeding on the mudflats. Amongst them black-tailed godwits and ringed plovers scurry about, depending on the time of year. You might be lucky to see brent-geese, found between November and April. On our brief spell of bird-watching we saw plenty of duck and curlew.

About 4 km from Drogheda you will come to a sign for Beaulieu House, pronounced Bewley, like the old nostalgic café in Grafton Street. Detour a little left to see this architectural gem. Originally the Plunketts of Beaulieu owned the lands and a manor here. It was confiscated during the Cromwell period and eventually obtained by Sir Henry Tichborne. He built the current house in the mid 1600s, which was probably influenced by Dutch architecture. Sir Henry was also famous for defending Drogheda successfully, during the rebellion of 1641, against the Irish army led by Phelim O'Neill. In the adjacent cemetery there is a church and two interesting medieval stone tomb-covers. One is particularly macabre, depicting a skeleton. It appears that the figure is in a state of decomposition. Cadavers such as this may have been influenced by memories of corpses during the Black Plague. On the day we were there the house and cemetery were closed; however, we could see the tomb-covers from the cemetery gate. Beaulieu House is a private residence and only open to the public at certain times.

Return to the R167 and cycle 2 km to a sign for Baltray, detour right following the sign. At a pub called the 19th, turn left and then right up a track. You should dismount here, as the ground can be muddy. Just past the second house is an entrance to a field on the right. To the left of the entrance, near to what looks like a water tower, can be seen two ancient standing stones. A recent claim puts them in context. It seems that the flat part of the larger stone is in line with Rockabill, two granite islands about 24 km out to sea; the larger island has a lighthouse on it. Apparently during the winter solstice around 21 December, the sun rises near Rockabill at the same angle as the line of the stone, similar to the phenomenon at Newgrange. This was indeed Stone Age genius and these ancient men or women devised it without computers, incredible! Moving on, if you are a keen golfer you might like to check out the host of the 2004 Irish Open — County Louth Golf Club is one of the top courses in the country and located just beyond the 19th Pub.

Cycle back to the R167 and onwards to Termonfeckin, 2 km away. This is a charming village shaded by broadleaved trees. A river flows nice and easy through its centre, reflecting the mood of the place.

Ecclesiastical periods in particular have influenced local history. Termonfeckin gets its name from St Feckin who founded a monastery here around the 7th century. It was also home to the medieval and later Protestant primates until the 17th century. There are 2 fine, old churches in the town. As you enter from Baltray you will pass the RC Church of the Immaculate Conception, built in 1883. In the centre of the town is St Feckin's Church of Ireland, built in 1792. The only remaining artefact of the ancient monastery, a decorated high cross, stands amongst the tombstones in the cemetery surrounding the church. Near the town centre is a sign for Seapoint Golf Club. A small detour in this direction will present Termonfeckin Castle. This is a fortified tower house built to protect its wealthy owners, the 15th-century equivalent to alarms and surveillance cameras. In remarkable condition, the house has 3 storeys accessed by a spiral staircase. The corbelled roof is similar in design to the roof in Newgrange passage grave, built 5,000 years before. The house is associated with the Brabazon family, and Archbishop Robert Ussher, the famous antiquarian, was a neighbour. There are lovely views from the roof and a key for entry is available by calling to the bungalow opposite.

Leave the town on the R166 to Clogherhead, about 4 km away. The coast will come into view again. About 1 km from Clogherhead, to your left, is the ruin of Glaspistol Castle covered in dead ivy. St Oliver Plunkett spent time here before being arrested and hung, drawn and quartered on trumped-up charges of treason. Continue into the village. Clogherhead was always a popular holiday resort as can be seen by the number of mobile homes in the area. It's probably less popular now that sunny destinations abroad have become more affordable. Detour right to Port Oriel, about 1 km downhill. Originally built in 1885, it consists of a pier and sheltered harbour for the fishing boats. There are fine views along the north coast to the Mourne Mountains. Fishing off the pier is a popular pastime but there was no one here on the day we visited. However, there were other very proficient exponents in the form of four grey seals swimming leisurely near the pier. Their horsy-type snouts made them very conspicuous.

Cycle back up the hill to Clogherhead and turn right onto the R166 again. About 1 km from the village is a rustic, old church. Continue to the next crossroads, Murray's Cross, about 3 km away. Turn left, at a 12-km signpost for Drogheda, onto this third-class road. At about

2 km are the remains of an old petrol pump. I wondered how they ever did business here. After passing through a shaded stretch of road you will arrive at Blackhall. There is a fine, old church on your right with a castellated bell tower. Beyond this is farming country as evidenced by the number of farms and agricultural odours. Just before you join with the R166 again there is a thatched cottage to your right. At the junction with the R166 turn right for Drogheda, 4 km away. Soon you will enter the outskirts of the town and see the arched railway bridge with the Magdalene Tower in the background. This is the remains of a 14th-century Dominican friary. Pass under the bridge and continue to a fire station on your left. Take the second left turn after the fire station at a sign for the town centre, before the Magdalene Tower. Cycle down the hill and at the bottom go left again under St Laurence's Gate. This is the last surviving gate of 10, a part of the medieval walls of Drogheda. It is actually a barbican, an outer defence. Having passed under the gate turn immediately right and then left in the direction of Baltray. Continue under the viaduct once more, back to your car.

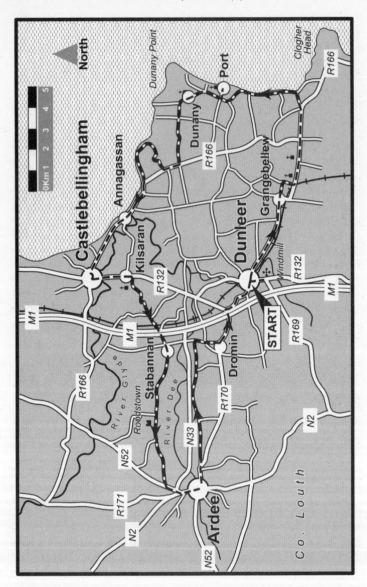

24. Lugh's County (Louth)

Distance (km)	61
Cycling time (hours)	$5^3/4$
Terrain	Rolling (verges on)
Roads (OSI 36 map)	Three-quarters on third-class, the remainder on regional
Attractions	Coast, Mountain views, Heritage

Louth gets its name from Lugh, the ancient god of the Celts. This cycle follows a route through central Louth, and is mainly an easy one. The county was the main setting of an epic tale, Tain Bo Cuailgne, and the route takes in a little of the substantial Tain Cycling Trail. The route begins at Dunleer and heads for the coast through Grangebellew. After, it follows close to the shoreline passing the sandy beach at Port Lurganboy before heading inland on tranquil back roads. It emerges at the coast again at Annagassan, where views of the Mournes and particularly the Cooley Mountains are magnificent. The route then turns inland to Castlebellingham whose name originates from a captain in Cromwell's army. It then passes through very pleasant countryside to Ardee, where the legendary Ulster hero Cuchulainn fought in single combat with his foster brother Ferdia. The final section is a relaxing cycle back to Dunleer.

From the City, take the M1 past Drogheda to the exit for Dunleer. Follow the signs into the town centre where you should find parking. The town is about 65 km from Dublin.

Cycle through Dunleer towards Dublin. About 0.5 km past the Clogherhead junction, you should see a sign for a mill. Detour left here down a track. This is Whiteriver Mill known locally as Connor's Mill. It is a water-powered, 18th-century mill, still in use. Visitors are welcome, and there is an entry fee. Return back in the direction of town, and at the junction for Clogherhead turn right onto the R170. After cycling by fertile, rolling fields for about 5 km you arrive at the crossroads at Grangebellew. Continue straight across, leaving the R170. Turn right at the T-junction about 0.5 km away. On your left is Rath Cemetery and the remains of an old church belfry. Behind you in the near distance is another old tower, a folly or windmill perhaps. I asked some locals how it came about, but they were unable to tell me except that that it may have originated from Barmeath Castle, the remains of which are nearby. Sadly there have been a number of tragic accidents caused by falls from the tower.

Continue on past the cemetery to the R170, and turn left. After 2 km you will pass an unusual church with a square belfry attached to a taller, castellated tower. Continue past a crossroads and take the second left towards the sea, about 1 km away. You will arrive at a yield sign; turn left here and soon you will be cycling along the shoreline. Ahead in the distance are the Cooley and Mourne Mountains; the small headland is Dunany Point. The cliffs at Dunany are of yellow clay and this was used locally for minor building repairs before cement was available. Also along here is Port Lurganboy Beach, a sandy beach with no stones. Soon after, the road veers away from the shoreline. Detour at the first turn right to Port, about 1.5 km after leaving the shoreline. There are ruins of a medieval church situated in the cemetery here. There is also one to be found at Dunany. It would appear that there was once a thriving religious community in the area.

Return to the main road and turn right. Take the next left following the sign for the scenic route. Pass Dunany Church on the right and soon the road veers sharply to the left. Continue to the R166 and turn right, following the signs for Annagassan, 4 km away. As you approach the village the sea comes into view again. Pass through the village to a bridge where the combined waters of the Rivers Glyde and Dee pass under. About 0.5 km upstream is where the two rivers confluence. Just before crossing the bridge, take a detour right to a small harbour sheltering small fishing boats. There are picnic tables here. Looking from the end of the pier you can see Dundalk and behind is the peak of Black Mountain, rising to 508 m. Scanning right is Carlingford Mountain, and the Mountains of Mourne sweeping down to the sea.

Return to the main road, R166, and cross the bridge. The road turns inland on the Tain Trail towards Castlebellingham. The Tain Trail Cycling Route is about 585 km long and starts at Rathcroghan in County Roscommon. It follows quite closely the epic saga of the Cattle Raid of Cooley. This ancient tale recounts the quest of Queen Maeve of Connaught to capture the Tain Bo Cuailgne or Brown Bull of Cooley. Her aim was to match the great white bull of her husband's. Cuchulainn alone defends the Brown Bull and Ulster from Maeve's armies, as his fellow warriors are held under a sleeping spell. Maeve eventually captures the Brown Bull, but the Ulster warriors awaken and drive her armies back. The Brown Bull meets with the White Bull and both fight to their deaths, ending the bloody tale.

Continue to Castlebellingham about 4 km away. This town was largely constructed by the Bellingham family whose ancestor was a captain in Cromwell's army. He was granted confiscated lands here in the 1650s. The current Bellingham Castle Hotel, dated c. 18th century, is situated on the site of the old castle, and there is a fine castellated gateway leading to it. In the town turn left onto the main street in the direction of Dunleer. The hotel is on your right beyond the town centre. You will pass over the River Glyde on leaving the town. Kilsaran is only 1.5 km away. Here take the first right just past St Mary's Church, the belfry of which was erected in 1856. This road to Stabannan, about 4 km, provides pleasant cycling through partially-wooded countryside. As you approach the village you will cycle under the main Dublin/Belfast railway line and the M1 motorway. At the yield sign turn left and then right at the Cross Bar Pub. Pass the RC church, and at the edge of town, on the left, is the cemetery and remains of a belfry built in 1826. Here the country opens a fine view to the left and as you ascend the view gets better, eventually spreading to the right as well. About 3 km from Stabannan is Roodstown Castle. This is a fine example of a fortified tower house owned by 15th- or 16th-century landowners. These tower houses were popular within the Pale and provided protection for the owners during the turbulent times then. The entrance lobby is protected by a murder hole. It allowed the defendants to fire on attackers as they came through the door. This country home stands in stark contrast to the modern bungalows surrounding it now.

About 5 km passed Roodstown is a junction with the N52. Turn left into Ardee, following the signs. At the second roundabout note the sculpture on the right, looking like the helmet of an ancient warrior. Ardee was founded by a Norman knight, de Pippard, who obtained a grant of entitlement from Prince John c. 1185.

But the town's association with Cuchulainn goes back further. Ardee means 'Ferdia's ford on the River Dee'. During the Tain Bo Cuailgne, Cuchulainn fought his former comrade Ferdia here. Ferdia was now the champion of Maeve's warriors. During the deadly combat lasting four days, both men displayed acts of courtesy and chivalry. Eventually Cuchulainn mortally wounded Ferdia, and in a final courtesy carried Ferdia's body to the north bank of the Dee, a symbolic act after Ferdia had fought in vain to capture the north bank. Cycle to the River Dee on the far side of town. On the right of the road in a car park is a monument to Cuchulainn and Ferdia.

Cross over the river and turn left onto the R170 in the direction of Dunleer. Continue straight ahead onto a third-class road in the direction of Richardstown, leaving the R170. This road runs in parallel to the one you came in on. So you will see Roodstown Castle off to the left as you cycle. Finally after 6 km, the road leads to a junction at Kaigs Cross, turn right for Dromin. Almost immediately the church steeple at Dromin comes into view. At the next junction take the second left, the road faces you. Cycle past the old church, and turn left onto the R170. Continue under the motorway and cross the roundabouts, following the signs for Dunleer, about 1 km away. Back in the town centre you could have a relaxing snack in a choice of local establishments before heading home.

25. COOLEY PENINSULA (LOUTH, ARMAGH)

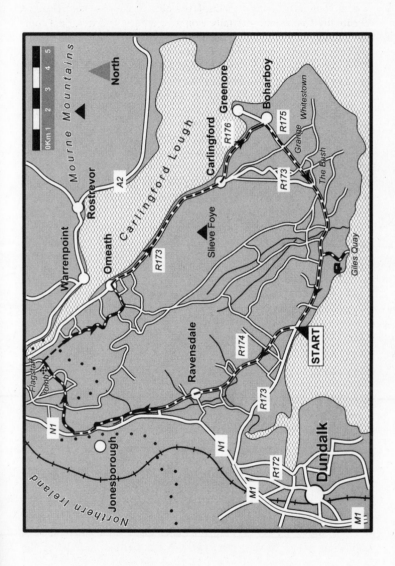

25. Cooley Peninsula (Louth, Armagh)

Distance (km)	48
Cycling Time (Hrs)	$5^1/_4$
Terrain	Hilly
Roads (osi 36 map)	Three-quarters on regional, remaining third-class except for 1 km on N1
Attractions	Mountain, Forest, Lough, Coast, Heritage

The beautiful Cooley Peninsula is abundant with legendary tales of Cuchulainn, Fionn Mac Cumhaill and more, and it has what I believe to be one of the finest views in Ireland. Consequently the route is partially hilly but not over the top, if you will excuse the pun. It starts at Dundalk Bay in County Louth and passes through the Flurry River valley on the southern side of the Cooley Mountains. After crossing into County Armagh the route climbs to Flagstaff which offers the most magnificent views over Carlingford Lough. Then follows a descent back over the border to Omeath, and continues hugging the Lough shore on the northern side of the Cooleys to the heritage town of Carlingford. For such a small town Carlingford is well furnished with evidence of its medieval past. Finally the route heads back towards your car taking a detour to the 19th-century harbour of Giles Quay on the way.

From Dublin take the M1 beyond Dundalk to the roundabout at the end of the motorway. Follow the signs back towards Dundalk. At the next roundabout turn left onto the R173 following the sign for Carlingford. Drive for about 7 km to the junction with the R174 at a sign for Ravensdale. You can park your car off-road, just past the junction.

Cycle onto the R174 towards Ravensdale, 6 km away. The road rises gradually towards this picturesque village set on the southern slopes of the Cooley Mountains. Behind you is Dundalk Bay gaping at the Irish Sea. After about 4 km you come to a sign for the Tain Way. This 40-km walking circuit, from Ravensdale to Carlingford through the mountains, follows some of the exploits of Queen Maeve and Cuchulainn in the epic tale, Tain Bo Cuailgne or Cattle Raid of Cooley. It was to the right of here in the mountains that Queen Maeve and her armies lay waste to the countryside in her frenzied search for the

Brown Bull of Cooley, hidden in the mountains. Cuchulainn defends the prized bull alone as his fellow warriors lie asleep under a spell. Eventually Maeve captures the animal and leaves for home. But the saga is far from over. After many more bloody battles her husband's great White Bull and the Brown Bull fight a mighty battle themselves. The Brown Bull emerges victorious but mortally wounded. He returns to the Cooleys with the remains of the White Bull on his horns, only to die. You might like to consider doing the Tain Trail Cycling Route sometime. It is a lot more substantial than the Tain Way, 585 km in fact. Generally it follows Queen Maeve's route from her royal residence in Rathcroghan, County Roscommon, to the Cooley Mountains and back.

Continue to Ravensdale, 3 km from the Tain Way sign. About 1.5 km past the village, the R174 turns to the left. Cycle straight onto a minor road into forested area, Ravensdale Wood actually. The Flurry River is down to your left, and on its outside is the main N1 road to the North. Follow the minor road for about 3.5 km until it comes to a junction with the very busy N1. Turn right for about 1 km to a sign indicating Omeath, passing the Carrickdale Hotel on the way. There are some paths along here that you could choose to walk on rather than compete with traffic on the road. At the Omeath sign turn right. The road climbs into Armagh which is about 1.5 km from the N1. Soon after is Clontygora Court Tomb, signposted to the right and just off the road. This court tomb was built by Neolithic farmers. Although extensively damaged, the tomb consisted of a U-shaped court or open area which led through large portal stone slabs to burial chambers. The funeral rites may have taken place in the court area before the remains were taken to the chambers for burial. For some reason court tombs are more prevalent in northern parts of the country.

Return to the road and cycle on to Flagstaff, about 2 km from the tomb on your left. This viewing and picnic area presents a magnificent panorama of Carlingford Lough, sheltered by the Mourne Mountains in the north and the Cooleys in the south. The town of Warrenpoint can be seen directly below. It is a lovely setting for a picnic on a fine day. After viewing return to the main road and continue downhill to a crossroads, about 2 km away. Turn to the right here. The road levels out to a Y-junction. Keep left following the sign for the Oriel Trail, and at the next T-junction turn left onto a main road. The road descends into Omeath, altogether about 6 km from Flagstaff. The village gets its name from the Celtic tribe Ui Meith and was a native-Irish-speaking district, but alas no more. Across the Lough is the busy harbour at Warrenpoint, originating from the 1770s.

At the junction with the R173, turn right towards Carlingford, about 7 km away. On the outskirts of Omeath you will pass on the left a shrine to St Jude, the patron saint of hopeless cases, and in my case worth a stop. Continuing, the town of Rostrevor is to your left across the lough, and Slieve Foye ahead to your right. Some say that this mountain is actually the sleeping giant Fionn Mac Cumhaill, his slumbering bulk outlined by the shape of the mountain and beyond. Amongst his many exploits, the legendary giant threw a sod of earth out to sea which became the Isle of Man, enabling a thriving ferry business for the future. About halfway to Carlingford is Slieve Foye Wood on the right and close to Carlingford, a marina of yachts with rattling halyards. As you enter the town you cross under a bridge by King John's Castle. This Norman fortress commands a strong position over the harbour, and is accessed from the harbour. Although called King John's Castle, it was built by Hugh de Lacy c. 1200. However, King John is attributed to have stayed here for a few days. From the harbour turn right into the town centre. The small castle you see near the car park is Taaffe's Castle, now connected to more modern buildings. This was probably built c. 15th century and is an example of a defensive town house, equipped with such useful features as slit windows for firing muskets, and a murder hole. Within the town are the Mint and Tholsel. The Mint is a 15th-century building reflecting the prosperity of Carlingford at the time, as the town was granted a licence to mint coinage. At the end of the pedestrian way is the Tholsel, a medieval customs barrier used to prevent untaxed goods from entering the town. Later it became a gaol.

Return to the main road and turn right onto the R176 to continue along the lough shore. After 4 km you will come to a junction with the R175. Turn right onto it. Another 4 km will take you to Bush Church on the left. Continue past for 3 km to a left turn for Giles Quay, an anchor marks the spot. A 3-km detour will take you there and back. A popular holiday resort, the approach to the 19th-century pier presents a pretty picture. Return to the main road and continue cycling through Lordship, after which Dundalk Bay comes into view and soon after you will return to your car, about 4 km from the Giles Quay turn. On

your drive back towards Dundalk, you could take a break in the
Ballymascanlon House Hotel, an old Victorian house. The 3,000-year-
old Proleek Dolmen, a portal tomb, is in the grounds.

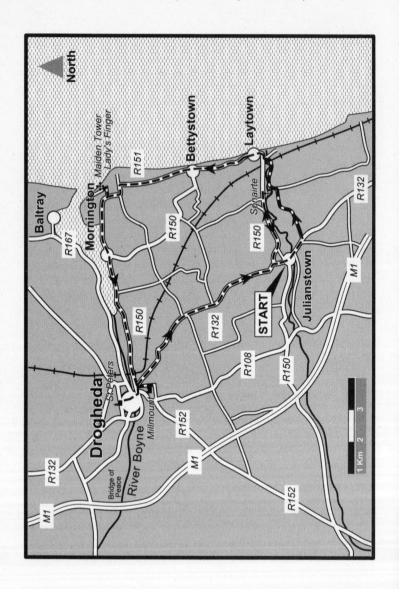

North

Baltray

R167

R132

M1

Drogheda

St Peters

Bridge of Peace

River Boyne

Millmount

R152

M1

Mornington

Maiden Tower
Lady's Finger

R151

Bettystown

Laytown

R132

Sonairte

R150

R150

R150

R132

START

Julianstown

R108

R150

R150

M1

R152

1 Km   2   3

Distance (km)	32
Cycling time (hours)	3
Terrain	Flat
Roads (OSI 43 map)	Mainly regional, some third-class, busy stretch on R132 (old N1) for 7 km
Attractions	Coast, Rivers, Heritage

This easy cycle, crossing the borders of Meath and Louth, is characterised by water. It follows the small River Nanny from Julianstown to where it enters the sea at Laytown. The route then covers half of the tiny coastline of Meath. Here, there are fine views along the coast from the broad beaches of Laytown and Bettystown. Eventually it reaches the Boyne Estuary where Ireland's earliest inhabitants would have navigated, and evidence of old maritime markers can be seen. The route then continues upstream along the south bank of the Boyne to the medieval town of Drogheda with memories of its two Olivers — the saint, Oliver Plunkett, and the soldier, Oliver Cromwell. The return journey takes in an ecology centre just before finishing back at Julianstown.

Take the M1 north past Balbriggan and exit onto the R132 (old N1) for Julianstown. Follow the signs to the village; it is about 40 km from the City. After passing the 50-kph speed restriction you will see a school on your right, park in this area.

On the Dublin side of the school there is a third-class road. Start your cycle on this, passing a church on the left. This modern church has a type of contemporary Gothic entrance and window, quite unusual I thought. At about 1.5 km there is a modern wind generator far over to your left and in contrast some old ruins to your right. Shortly after you will come to a T-junction, turn left here. Soon the River Nanny will come into full view. Follow it for about 1 km to a wooden footbridge. Dismount and cross the bridge. Be careful, as the wood can be slippery when wet. On your right is the larger bridge carrying the Dublin–Belfast railway line and busy commuters to and from work. Having crossed the footbridge, cross the railway station car park into Laytown and the coastal part of the cycle begins. As you veer left onto the beach road (R151), notice the sculpture called Voyager on your right by artist Linda Brunker.

The twin towns of Laytown and Bettystown have been popular seaside resorts for years, especially for people from Drogheda and Dublin. Today they are growing commuter towns. Laytown is famous for its horseracing tradition. The race is unique because it is held on the strand at low tide and a temporary grandstand is erected on the sand dunes. You can imagine the excitement of the punters when the thundering hooves of the thoroughbreds whip up the sea sand as they race for glory. Then afterwards the tide's wide sweep washes away all evidence of the contest for another year. The race was established in 1901 and nothing, not even 2 world wars, has stopped it since.

After 3 km you will arrive in Bettystown with the refurbished Neptune Hotel on your right. The Tara Brooch was found on the beach here in 1850 and is an exceptional example of early Christian art in Ireland. The story goes that a poor woman looking for driftwood on the beach found it. Initially she had difficulty selling the artefact as it was regarded as worthless. But eventually its importance was recognised and it is now in the National Museum in Dublin. Admiring the beach on a sharp St Stephen's Day, I witnessed a bunch of hardy souls dash into the uninviting sea for charity. I thought I was brave cycling on such a day, but these people were truly heroic. Brrrr, I would have waited till summer.

Cycle past Bettystown Golf Club, a links course where players have the luxury of natural sand bunkers and where the occasional sharp northeasterly would slice a player's ball. Continue on the R151 and take a short detour at the second turn to your right, about 2 km from the golf club. Here you can view the River Boyne entering the sea with its ancient and modern navigation beacons. The 2 old ones here are the Lady's Finger and Maiden Tower with its castellated top. The Maiden Tower gets its name from the unmarried Elizabeth I of England. Nothing much is known of the Lady's Finger. I suppose it could have been a symbolic gesture to one of the many invaders.

Return to the R151 and continue; it becomes the R150 as you cycle upstream along the banks of the Boyne to the nearby village of Mornington. Past Mornington, the features of Drogheda appear, dominated by the arches of the 19th-century railway viaduct across the Boyne. Look across the river for a fine old residence called Beaulieu

House. It was originally a Jacobean manor, built *c*. 1628. Eventually you will pass under one of the viaduct's arches, and after 1 km come to a set of traffic lights. Turn right, crossing over the Boyne toward the town centre, and then left. Follow the one-way system eventually turning right at the Dominican church and shortly after right again into busy West Street. As you cycle along West Street you will soon come to St Peter's Church on your left, a fine neo-Gothic example built in the 1880s. The head of the martyr and saint, Oliver Plunkett, is enshrined here, along with some other remains. He was born in Loughcrew, County Meath, and was appointed Archbishop of Armagh and Primate of All-Ireland in 1669. He founded a school in Drogheda for Catholic and Protestant boys run by the Jesuits. He was hung, drawn and quartered in 1681 on trumped-up charges of treason in London, the last Catholic to suffer martyrdom in Ireland.

On leaving the church continue on West Street to the Tolsel, an 18th-century building adorned with a 4-faced clock. Turn right here and cross over the Boyne again, this is the same bridge you crossed when entering the town. At the traffic lights, cycle left in the direction of Dublin. At the next lights turn right at a sign for Millmount. Follow the signs to this old fort, now a museum perched high on a hill. Its location presents fine views over Drogheda. Millmount offered Oliver Cromwell fierce resistance at the siege of Drogheda in 1649. At that time Cromwell was sent to Ireland to quash Royalist resistance, especially in Ulster. He identified Drogheda as a key strategic location in his campaign. Then the formidable walls, ruins of which remain today, protected the town. They were about 6 m high, and 2 m thick at the bottom, narrowing to the top. Eventually the walls were breached and the defenders driven to Millmount to make a last stand. The garrison was offered quarter, but when they surrendered none was given. They were massacred and it was said that the commander, Sir Arthur Aston, was beaten to death with his own wooden leg. The scene after was horrendous as Cromwell's soldiers, following his orders, massacred thousands in the town — men, women and children. The effect of this broke the Royalist morale in the northeast and they capitulated quickly. Apparently this type of dreadful deed was common in sieges at the time. But it was no excuse for Cromwell; he continues to remain infamous in Drogheda.

Return to the R132 (old N1) and cycle to Julianstown, about 7 km away in the Dublin direction. Just before Julianstown, if you feel up to it, detour left onto the R150 passing St Mary's Church on your left. Continue to the Sonairte Ecology Centre, about 2 km away. Sonairte, meaning 'positive strength', is a place for environmental education and promotion. It contains almost 7 acres, which includes a nature trail, an organic garden and an energy park. Opening times vary depending on time of year. Return to the R132 (old N1) and cycle through the village back to your car. If you are feeling peckish or thirsty, Julianstown has a thatched pub and a hotel in the village. The hotel was built on the site of a 200-year-old flour mill beside the River Nanny.

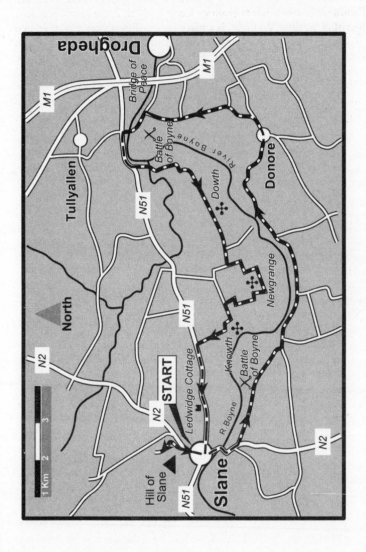

Distance (km)	32
Cycling time (hours)	$4^1/_2$
Terrain	Mainly rolling, hilly at Hill of Slane
Roads (osi 43 map)	Busy stretch on N51 for 3 km and N2 for 1 km, otherwise third-class roads
Attractions	River, Ledwidge (poet) museum, plenty of Heritage

It's easy to see why Stone-Age man chose the Boyne Valley for his most important and impressive buildings. The area is truly beautiful and steeped in history. You too will be impressed as you cycle through the lush countryside, following tree-lined roads that suddenly reveal magnificent views. You can marvel at the architectural genius of the ancient passage graves at Bru na Boinne. Or imagine the mood when St Patrick lit his paschal fire near Slane in 433 AD, in spite of the pagan king, Laoghaire. If you prefer your history a little more modern, you can review the military tactics of James II and William of Orange at the Battle of the Boyne near Donore. Could James have retreated faster if he had a bicycle? These natural and heritage gems sit by the meandering waters of the Boyne. Through this area the river makes a great horseshoe that surely influenced all that took place here. Enjoy it.

Take the N2 to Slane about 45 km from the City. About 1 km from the town, there is a parking area on your right. It's before the traffic lights controlling traffic over the bridge; you can park your car here. Cycle back in the Dublin direction on the N2 for about 100 m and then turn left at a sign for the Battle of the Boyne. It's a pleasure to get off the busy N2 here and hear the birds sing. The River Boyne will be to your left on this third-class road but it soon meanders away. After 1.5 km, watch for the heritage sign describing the flanking tactic by the Williamite forces at the Battle of the Boyne. It successfully forced the Jacobites to send a large detachment from the main theatre at Oldbridge, leaving them vastly outnumbered at this crucial position.

After 3 km, turn left at a T-junction, again following the signs for the Battle of the Boyne (Oldbridge House). Soon the River Boyne comes back into view through the trees lining the road. It has carved a semi-circle in under 2 km. After 1 km look for a car park on the left. You can choose to detour here on a path by the Boyne. It runs for about 2 km before returning to the main road at a pumping station. There is a great view of Newgrange from it. Continue on the main road to Bru na Boinne (Palace of the Boyne) Interpretative Centre. Here you can learn about the passage graves of Newgrange, Knowth and Dowth and take a conducted tour. The full tour lasts about 2 hours. These ancient monuments were built over 5,000 years ago and are a wonder of engineering and art. Newgrange is famous for its winter solstice, which lasts for 17 minutes at dawn from the 19th to the 23rd of December. The sun shines through a roof box and along a passage to light up the main chamber, representing rebirth and life. How advanced can you get? The Celts also recognised this as a special place and it's said that the celebrated Cuchulainn was conceived here. Having fortified your mind with knowledge, you can fortify your body by having coffee and sticky cake in the café or perhaps something less enjoyable but healthier. Although the cycle will take you by the burial mounds, visitors are permitted on the sites through the Interpretative Centre only. Dowth is the exception; here you can enter the site.

On exiting Bru na Boinne, turn left towards Drogheda. You will soon come to the village of Donore, 2 km away. As you cycle into the village there is a pretty, thatched cottage on the right, it was for sale the day I passed. Cycle through the village to another thatched cottage called 'The Boyne Valley Cottage'. One of its walls contains a mural of the Battle of the Boyne. Memories of the event are probably in its ancient walls too. Turn left here following the signs for the Battle of the Boyne (Oldbridge House); it's about 4 km from Donore. This is where the main clash occurred, although it's difficult to imagine the chaotic images and din of battle in this tranquil place. William's crack, Dutch troops were positioned at several fords north of the river. They charged across and although fiercely opposed by Irish cavalry, triumphed through superior firepower and greater numbers. Their success was James's folly. He had sent too many troops upstream to cut off the Williamite flanking movement, leaving this place thinly defended. James did not hang around after; he fled to France leaving the Irish in the lurch. And of course his legacy lives on today. The battle site is open for tours from May to September.

Continue over the Boyne at Oldbridge to the junction with the N51 and turn left in the direction of Slane. After 1 km turn left off the N51, towards the passage graves at Newgrange, Knowth and Dowth. As you cycle way from the junction notice the road sign to be beware of leaping deer. Continue for about 2 km through tree-lined roads and you will see Dowth Castle on your left. John Boyle O'Reilly, journalist and republican, was born here in 1844. He was arrested for treason and eventually sent to Australia from where he escaped to America. There he became a successful journalist and publisher.

Just past the John Boyle O'Reilly Memorial is the passage grave of Dowth, the least known of the three tombs of Bru na Boinne. Visitors cannot enter the tomb although they can walk around the site. Notice a large crater in the centre of the mound caused by poorly-planned excavations in the 1840s. The tomb has two main chambers facing westwards and there are smaller tombs to the east and southwest of the large mound. The views from here are beautiful and it's understandable why our ancestors should choose this site.

Cycle on for about 1 km to a T-junction, turn left and follow the sign for Newgrange Farm. Soon the majestic tomb of Newgrange comes into view with its white quartz frontage facing the waters of the Boyne not far below. This is the best known of the three tombs, with its winter solstice wonder. The mound consists of a single tomb and there are remains of other tombs nearby. Just past the mound is Newgrange Farm. Here visitors can experience a working farm, except during winter when it is closed. Continuing on, the road veers to the right and narrows. Traffic can be busy on this stretch especially during peak tourist periods, so be careful. After 1 km you will come to a T-junction. Turn left here and after another kilometre you will come to Knowth, the 3rd of the three tombs of Bru na Boinne. Like Newgrange, visitors are only permitted on the site through the Interpretative Centre. As well as two passage tombs within the mound, Knowth also contains fascinating examples of Neolithic art. Follow the road to the N51 junction not far away. Turn left towards Slane. This national secondary route is busy and quite narrow, so be cautious. Near the town of Slane, to the right on a bend, is the Francis Ledwidge Cottage and Museum. Born here in 1887, this First World War soldier and poet was killed in 1917 in Belgium. The cottage is open to visitors all year round.

Cycle on to the centre of Slane. Detour right and take the sign-posted turn left for the Hill of Slane. A steep climb is rewarded by magnificent views from the top. According to legend, it was on this hill in 433 AD that St Patrick lit the first paschal fire in Ireland. King Laoghaire saw the fire from his palace at Tara and regarded it as an act of defiance against his own pagan gods. However, Patrick had the gift of the gab and although Laoghaire remained a pagan himself, he permitted Patrick to preach to his subjects. Return to the village and continue towards the bridge passing Slane Castle, now better known for open-air concerts. Some of the greats played here such as U2, the Rolling Stones and Bruce Springsteen. Cross the narrow bridge, controlled by traffic lights, and climb the hill up to your car.

28. Ceanannas Mor (Meath, Westmeath)

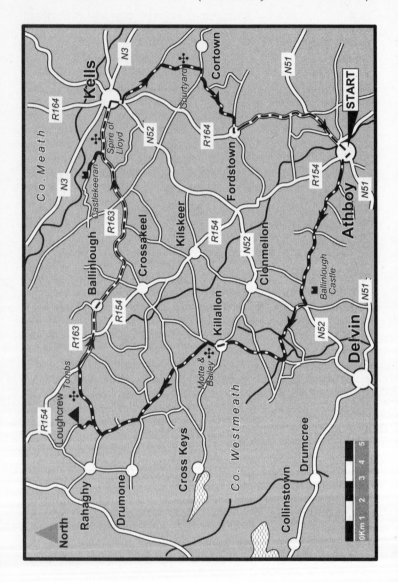

Distance (km)	67
Cycling time (hours)	$5^3/4$
Terrain	Hilly at Loughcrew, otherwise rolling
Roads (OSI 42 map)	Three-quarters on third-class, the rest on regional except for about 2 km on N51 and N52
Attractions	Scenic hills, Gardens, plenty of Heritage

This heritage route takes in the megalithic passage graves on the Loughcrew Hills near Oldcastle, and visits the source of the Book of Kells. *The ancient cairns at Loughcrew have not been developed like Newgrange and so remain relatively unspoilt. The hills on which they stand are the highest in the area and offer magnificent views across the surrounding countryside. This makes this part of the route quite hilly in contrast to the flatter terrain starting south.*

The route begins in the medieval town of Athboy before taking to pleasant and generally flat, country roads. Around Killallon the road begins to ascend, eventually climbing quite steeply up Slieve na Calliagh to the passage graves. Afterwards the route takes an easier road into Ceanannas Mor which makes a restful cycle after the previous vigour. Ceanannas Mor or Kells was an important monastic settlement whose legacy is the magnificent Book of Kells. *The route returns to Athboy on a mix of pleasant third-class and regional roads.*

From Dublin take the N3 in the direction of Navan. After Clonee, turn off the N3 onto the R154 for Trim. Continue to Trim and at the town continue to follow the R154 to Athboy. In Athboy turn left onto the main street. There is a car park just before the RC church on the right. Athboy is about 60 km from the City.

Once on your bicycle take the R154 in the direction of Oldcastle. After a short distance take a turn to the left following the sign for Ballinlough Castle Gardens. After 1 km is a Y-junction, keep right. Soon after you come to a village sign for Grennanstown, only to find there is very little here. After Grennanstown you cross the border into Westmeath. At the next crossroads cycle straight on, eventually reaching a sign for Ballinlough Castle Gardens and Golf Club, altogether about 8 km from Athboy. Turn left into the demesne. The 17th-century castle is the home of the Nugent family. The restored gardens are open to the public, and include lakeside and woodland walks. The walled garden is divided into four sections filled with herbaceous borders, a lily pond, a rose garden, and an herb and fruit garden. From the gardens you can access lakeside walks which present dramatic views of the castle. Ballinlough Castle Gardens are open weekends and bank holidays.

On leaving the demesne continue to the nearby junction with the N52. Turn right in the direction of Kells. Less than 1 km away the N52 turns sharply right, go left at the Y-junction here onto a third-class road. After 3 km you will come to a staggered crossroads at Graulty's Bridge. Turn right before the bridge and note that you are back in Meath again. Soon after, you will see the belfry of a white church in the distance before coming to a stop sign at a crossroads. Cycle straight across following the sign for Killallon, 2 km. You will pass the white church, built in 1837, on the right before finally entering the village. Take the second right at Killallon House. As you leave the village there is a motte on the left opposite the cemetery. The motte and bailey fort was an early Norman structure strategically located to defend a territory. They were made by digging a circular ditch and piling all the earth into the centre to form a conical, steep-sided mound. The summit of the mound was defended by a picket wall with a wooden tower inside. The bailey, an area enclosed by a picket oval ditch, was attached to improve defences. They were built from *c.* 1169 to *c.* 1230.

In less than 1 km you come to a left turn signposted for Oldcastle, take it. The road begins to rise gradually. Continue through the next crossroads, about 2 km away, following the sign for Oldcastle. After 3 km there is another crossroads, turn right here continuing to follow the sign for Oldcastle. The land becomes wooded with a mix of deciduous and coniferous trees and starts to descend. The hills around Loughcrew come into view on the right. About 2 km from the last crossroads is a stop sign at a T-junction onto a busier road, turn right. In less than 1 km there is a left turn for Loughcrew. Take this turn and almost immediately the road rises steeply, about 60 m over 1 km, to a car park. You may choose to walk some of it. From the car park you must walk to the passage graves. The Loughcrew Cairns form the largest set of passage graves in Ireland. They are megalithic structures, containing symbolic engravings dating from as far back as *c.* 4,000 BC and have astrological significance. There is evidence of various uses over time, but it is generally agreed that they were built as burial chambers. Because the area is currently undeveloped you can still enjoy the serene atmosphere and the fabulous views.

Return to the main road, taking care as you descend the steep hill, and turn left following the sign for the Boyne Drive. Follow the road for about 5 km to a junction with the Athboy road. Continue straight, on the R163, to Kells, 13 km away. Soon after is the village of Ballinlough with its unusual church equipped with two steeples. The road to Kells gets quite easy and you should make good progress. As you approach Kells the Spire of Lloyd comes into view. About 3 km from the town, you can take a 5-km round detour to Castlekeeran High Cross; the turn is signposted to the left. After about 2 km watch for a sign marked High Crosses and follow it crossing a field to the site. A monastery was founded here by St Ciaran who died around 770 AD. There are 3 badly-weathered high crosses here and the base of another. Apparently the cross of this base lies close by in the River Blackwater. Legend has it that St Columba was caught by St Ciaran taking the cross to his monastery at Kells, and so he dropped it in the river in his haste to get away.

Return to the main road and turn left towards Kells. In less than 1 km you come to People's Park on the left, and the Spire of Lloyd. This 18th-century mock lighthouse was built in memory of Sir Thomas Taylor by his son. There are also memorials to the poor of Kells who were buried here during the Great Famine. Cycle into Kells. Ceanannas Mor or Kells, meaning 'great fort', was known to be a royal place before St Colmcille founded a monastery here. As you enter the town the round tower and St Columba's Church are on the left — this was the site of St Colmcille's monastery. You can view St Colmcille's house from the back of the church site. Strange to see this 10th-century oratory set among modern bungalows. Four high crosses are found around St Columba's, although only the base remains of one. Of course Kells is famous for its book, now housed in Trinity College, Dublin. The scribes and artists who worked on the *Book of Kells* were likely to have been Columban monks. It is said that this highly-decorated manuscript, of the four gospels in Latin, was made over eleven hundred years ago. Copies of the book can be seen in St Columba's and the Heritage Centre.

28. Ceanannas Mor (Meath, Westmeath)

Continue to the centre of the town and the junction with the busy N52. Turn right in the direction of Mullingar. Cycle for about 0.5 km and then veer left onto the R164 for Athboy. Veer immediately left again off the R164 onto a third-class road. This is at the GAA park. After 3 km turn right and within 1 km you come to The Courtyard. The old stable and grounds of The Courtyard have been restored, and include craft and coffee shops set in pleasant garden surroundings. Cycle on to a T-junction near a cemetery and turn right in the direction of Fordstown, 3 km away. Soon after take a left turn following again the sign for Fordstown. At Fordstown turn left onto the R164 for Athboy, 6 km away. About halfway you pass a cross remembering those of the rebellion of 1798. Eventually the R164 becomes the N51 about 2 km from Athboy. Continue on this to the centre of town and back to your car. There are a number of places here to replenish and rest your tired muscles.

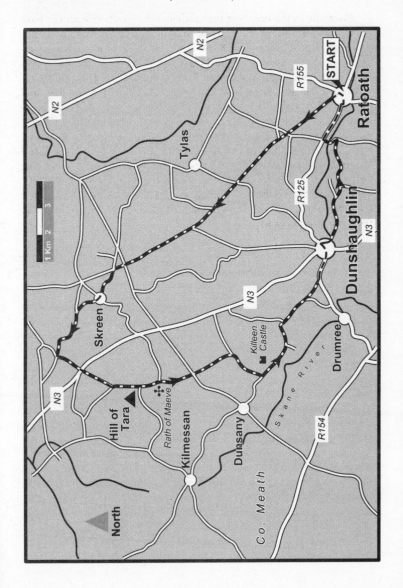

Distance (km)	39
Cycling time (hours)	4^1/$_2$
Terrain	Rolling
Roads (OSI 43 map)	Mainly third-class except for a 2-km stretch on the busy N3
Attractions	Scenic hills, Heritage

Tara fascinates archaeologists and historians alike and much has been written about it. The place itself does not have a great deal of visual antiquity. However, it is propounded to be a site of great ancient power and ritual, and more fascinating still is its mythical past. To top it all, the Hill of Tara commands one of the broadest views of any in this book.

The route is quite easy but for two energetic ascents, at the Hill of Skreen and at Tara itself. The first part of the route is rather nondescript, crossing flat grazing country. Eventually you will ascend to the village of Skreen where relics of St Colmcille were once kept. Then you continue to the Hill of Tara itself. Past Tara is the Rath of Maeve, an earthen ring fort. The route continues through the busy town of Dunshaughlin whose name derives from a nephew of St Patrick. Finally it follows a quiet country stretch before finishing back in Ratoath.

Take the N2 to within 1 km of Ashbourne and turn left at the sign to Ratoath. The town is about 25 km from the City. Turn right at the Holy Trinity Church, and park beside the cemetery.

Cycle on through the traffic lights in the direction of Skreen. On the day we passed, the road signs for Drogheda and Curragha were pointed incorrectly in our direction. This third-class road towards Skreen, sometimes spelt Skryne, is rather flat and uninteresting. We saw plenty of grazing sheep and horses, and at one stage a grey squirrel bounded alongside us in an adjacent field. At about 6 km from Ratoath, there is an attractive thatched house on the right. Three kilometres further, the road descends, and soon after you will come to a stop sign at a crossroads. Cross here to the next crossroads less than 1 km away, and turn left at the sign for Skreen. Soon you will see the old church on the top of the Hill of Skreen; head for it. The name Skreen derives from Colmcille's shrine. His shrine and relics were brought here in the 9th century. They were stolen in the 11th century by Norsemen, and apparently recovered later. The present church dates to the 15th century and there is an interesting effigy of a bishop over the door on the south side. The views from here are magnificent and you can see Tara over to the west. Generally the church is aligned east to west, with the tower looking west.

On leaving the site go left, away from O'Connell's Pub. Continue to a fork junction and veer left. The road descends to a crossroads. On the left is a cul-de-sac — if you fancy a break, detour here a short distance to a bridge crossing the River Gabhra, a pleasant place to relax for a while. Afterwards, return to the main road and continue to a T-junction. Turn left, and after 1 km you will meet a junction with the very busy N3. Unfortunately the route continues on this for about 2 km. Take the second right, following the sign for Tara, onto a third-class road and peace and quiet. The road ascends all the way to Tara, about 1 km.

Tara symbolises Irish tradition. The shamrock, the harp and gold brooches can all trace their way here. In myth, the Celtic sun-god Lug and fertility goddess Medhbh (Maeve) symbolised its royal greatness, and moved Ireland's high kings to rule from Tara. St Patrick was summoned here to explain himself after lighting his paschal fire at Slane, in spite of pagan king Laoghaire's ritual fire at Tara. He won the king over to Christianity using the shamrock to explain the Trinity. In more recent times the insurgents of 1798 and the Liberator Daniel O'Connell used Tara to symbolise their own messages. Audio-visual and guided tours at the site are available from mid-May to mid-September. However, it is open to walk about all year round, and there is a nice coffee shop as well. It is indeed a fascinating place and some say you can see 16 counties from the hill, in spite of its meagre 150-m height.

On leaving the site, turn right and pass the coffee shop following the sign for the Rath of Maeve. After 1.5 km you will arrive at this earthen fort on your right at a T-junction. It is dedicated to the goddess Maeve. She is associated with fertility and with the pagan festival Oimelg. The festival occurred at the beginning of February, heralding a time of fertility such as lambing and flowering. The site may well have been a ceremonial one celebrating spring.

Continue on through a crossroads to a T-junction. Turn right at the sign for Dunsany through a pleasant wooded area to another

T-junction. Turn left here at the sign for Dunshaughlin, 5 km away. Altogether you will have travelled about 3.5 km from the Rath of Maeve. Soon you will see the impressive Killeen Castle on your left, reputed to have had a window for every day of the year. The history of Killeen is a long one, stretching back to 1181 when the Norman, Geoffrey de Cusack, became lord of Killeen. He had assisted Hugh de Lacy in colonising Meath, whose lands were given to de Lacy by Henry II. The castle continued through a number of dynasties including a long line of Earls of Fingall. St Oliver Plunkett is reputed to have been related to the Fingalls and may have been educated at Killeen by Patrick Plunkett, who later became Bishop of Meath. In 1981 the castle was maliciously set on fire. It is now being developed into a hotel and golfing facility and hopefully will regain some of its former glory.

At the next T-junction turn left onto the R125 for Dunshaughlin, about 1 km. Eventually you will come to a stop sign in the town, turn right and look for the Church of Ireland on the left. St Seachnall founded his church on this site in the 5th century, and it is from him that the town gets its name, *Domhnach Seachnaill* or the Church of Seachnall. St Seachnall is reputed to have been a nephew of St Patrick, and arrived in Ireland from Gaul in 433 AD. The town continued to be a seat of Church power until the 12th century, after which it declined. However, Dunshaughlin has flourished in the last 20 years and its population has increased from around 400 to 4,000, about tenfold and counting.

After the church, take the first left and on the bend nearby veer right to Ratoath, 6 km away. Keep right at the cul-de-sac and continue straight, past the next T-junction. The cycle here is very pleasant and quiet. At the next T-junction, turn left over a small river. After 0.5 km you will meet with the junction at the R125. Turn right for Ratoath until you come to a stop sign. Then turn right and immediate left until you come to traffic lights. Turn right here back to your car.

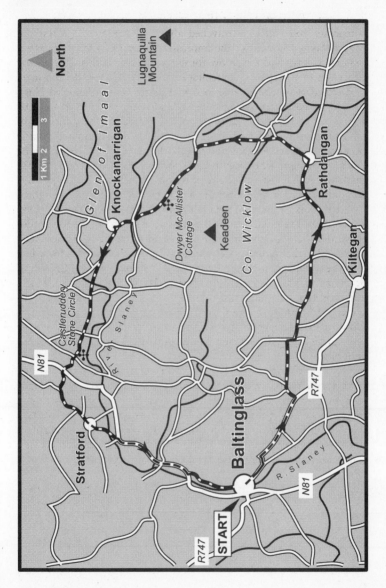

North

Lugnaquilla Mountain

Glen of Imaal

1 Km 2 3

Knockanarrigan

Dwyer McAllister Cottage

Keadeen

Co. Wicklow

Rathdangan

Kiltegan

Castleruddery Stone Circle

River Slaney

N81

Stratford

Baltinglass

R747

R. Slaney

N81

START

R747

Distance (km)	38
Cycling time (hours)	$4^1/_2$
Terrain	Mountainous
Roads (osi 55, 56, 61, 62 maps)	Mainly third-class except for 3 km on regional and 3 km on the N81
Attractions	Mountains, Woodland, River, Heritage

If, as is often said, Wicklow is the garden of Ireland then the Glen of Imaal must be its rockery. There is no shortage of rugged mountains and the Little Slaney and Slaney Rivers bubble through. But with all the lofty peaks, this route is by no means the most difficult in Wicklow.

It starts in the heritage town of Baltinglass with its 12th-century Abbey founded by the notorious Dermot McMurrough. It then heads on fairly level ground in the direction of Rathdangan. From here the route encounters the most difficult bit, the climb towards the Glen of Imaal. Near the Glen is the historic Dwyer McAllister cottage, where insurgents fought a battle with the Redcoats. The route then drops into the Glen to Knockanarrigan before turning west towards Stratford, built by an earl of the same name. Having passed through the village the route returns to picturesque Baltinglass.

Take the N81 from Dublin and follow the signs for Blessington. Drive through Blessington, continuing on the N81 to Baltinglass. The town is about 58 km from the City. In the centre of town turn left over the River Slaney onto the R747, and immediate left to Baltinglass Abbey. You can park by the Abbey.

Cycle back to the main road and turn left. Keep right of the 1798 memorial in the direction of Hacketstown. After 2.5 km you will pass a hospital on the left, take the next left turn 1 km further on, following the sign for Rathdangan, 9 km away. Soon after you will see a hill ahead whose tree-lined summit gives an impression of the head of a Mohican. Another 2.5 km will take you to a stop sign at a T-junction, turn right. Keep on the main road passing a church on the left. On your left are Keadeen and Carrig mountains which in turn are to the right of 'Mohican Head' mentioned previously. Another 1 km will take you to a Y-junction, keep right here. The route now passes through a deciduous wooded area whose trees embrace each other over the road, shading it and presenting a green tunnel through which you cycle; well, in summer anyway. After 1.5 km you come to a crossroads, go straight through. Soon after the view opens up, and the Wicklow Hills to the east emerge. Pass a left turn for Muckduff Lower and cycle over the Douglas River, Rathdangan is 1 km further.

It was in a church in Rathdangan that the local rebel leader Michael Dwyer and others attended mass one Sunday. The local yeomanry got wind of it and headed for the village. However, Dwyer had his own intelligence and word reached him that trouble was afoot. He organised some local farmers to climb a hill nearby, and when they caught sight of the yeomanry they called out. The militia gave chase thinking they were the rebels, allowing Dwyer and his men to escape.

At the crossroads in Rathdangan, turn left following the sign for the Dwyer McAllister Cottage, 8 km. The road now ascends, about 150 m over 4 km. On the way you will pass an animal sanctuary to the left called ASH. About 1.5 km from Rathdangan, keep left on a fork junction. Cycle past a cemetery and a set of crossroads. About 1 km past the fork junction is the beginning of a coniferous forest on the right, and a steep climb alongside. After a 2-km ascent the forest moves from right to left of the road, and the road itself begins to descend. Soon after you will come to a yield sign, keep left. Cycle for another 1.5 km to the Dwyer McAllister cottage, on the left. It is open during the summer months.

In the winter of 1799, Michael Dwyer, Samuel McAllister and two other rebels took refuge from the English in this cottage. The militia found out, and around 100 soldiers surrounded the cottage. A fierce gun fight took place. Sean McAllister was wounded and the two others killed. McAllister, realising his wounds would prevent him from escaping, stood at the doorway drawing fire, allowing Dwyer make his escape. Michael Dwyer continued fighting until 1803 when he finally surrendered and was deported to Australia.

Continue on from the Dwyer McAllister cottage for about 1.5 km where you cross over the Little Slaney River. Just past the river is a junction, go left following a sign for the Military Road. After 1 km you arrive at the crossroads at Knockanarrigan. Turn left here following the sign for Baltinglass. Cycle for about 4 km to the ancient Castleruddery Stone Circle on the left. The site consists of an earthen bank some 30 m in diameter, lined on the inside with upright stones. The entrance, to the south east, is marked by 2 large quartz boulders. There is also an outer perimeter, about 60 m in diameter, visible from the air only. This type of banked enclosure or henge was probably used for ceremonial purposes around 2,500 BC, and may also be linked to astronomical activity. There is no public access to the monument.

Cycle through the next crossroads and on to the junction with the N82. Cycle across to the third-class road opposite and over the Carrigower River. After less than 1 km you come to a T-junction, turn left at the yield sign for Stratford on Slaney, 1.5 km further and up a hill. The town originated from the aspirations of Edward Stratford whose ambition was to own a village that would bear his name. His family came from Stratford-upon-Avon. Edward, the 2nd Earl of Aldborough, laid out the village, building houses, shops and churches. He offered loans to people to settle there. Eventually he sold everything but the village continued to prosper and has survived to this day.

Cycle to the crossroads in the centre of Stratford. Turn right following the sign for Grange Con and then immediate left. The road descends out of Stratford and over the River Slaney to the N81. Turn right onto the N81 in the direction of Tullow. After 3 km you will come to a fork in the road, cycle left on the fork onto a third-class road. Another 2 km will take you back to Baltinglass and your car at the Abbey. The Cistercian Abbey here was founded by Dermot McMurrough, notorious for bringing the Anglo-Normans to Ireland. After Brian Boru's death at Clontarf in 1014, there was a leadership void in Ireland. An ongoing struggle for power between the chieftains ensued and Dermot, King of Leinster, was part of the tussle. However, his enemies the O'Rourkes and the Wexford Norsemen drove him out of Leinster. He crossed the water in search of help from Henry II of England. Henry was too busy at war with the French to get involved, but would later. In the meantime, Dermot succeeded in getting help from a powerful Norman in Wales, Richard Fitzgilbert de Clare, better known as Strongbow. Finally Norman war technology proved too much for the Irish and they capitulated. The country was to remain under English rule for another 800 years.

31. Blessington Lakes (Wicklow)

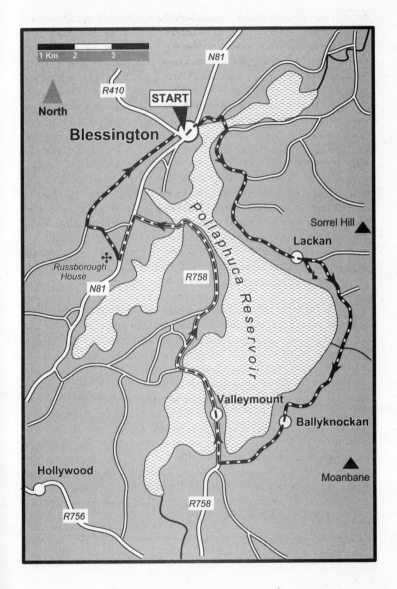

Distance (km)	31
Cycling time (hours)	$3^3/4$
Terrain	Rolling
Roads (OSI 56 map)	Two-thirds on third class, remainder on regional except for 1 km on N81
Attractions	Mountains, Lake, Forest, Heritage

Blessington Lakes are more correctly known as Poulaphouca Reservoir. These man-made lakes complement the magnificent surrounding features, and provide a range of leisure amenities too. Mountains surround the area; however, the route keeps fairly close to the water and so the gradients are not too taxing.

Starting at Blessington the route crosses the lakes and turns south towards Lackan, a hillside village overlooking this great expanse of water. The route continues to the charming Ballyknockan famous for its granite, and characteristically surrounded by stonewalled fields. Following on is Valleymount with an old church of unusual architecture. The route passes over the lakes again to the splendid Russborough House, a Palladian-style mansion and home of the famous Beit paintings. From here it's back to Blessington. Take something with you to eat, as you may not be able to buy food along the way, especially in winter.

From the M50 take exit 11 for the N81. Follow the signs for Blessington staying on the N81. The town is about 28 km from the City. You can park in the town centre by the monument to the Downshires. The town was built on lands granted to Archbishop Boyle *c.* 1667 and its name means town of blessing or gift. St Mary's Church, opposite the monument, dates from around the same time and there is a memorial there to Archbishop Boyle.

Once on your bike, cycle on past the hotel and turn left at the sign for Lackan, about 7 km from Blessington. Soon the arches of Blessington Bridge come into view. Descend to the bridge through a wooded area and after crossing turn right. The lake is to your right as you cycle towards Lackan. Blessington Lakes or more correctly Poulaphouca Reservoir is a man-made lake created as part of the River Liffey hydroelectric scheme started in the late 1930s. The shoreline runs for about 60 km and the lake is nearly 200 m above sea level. It is a means of flood control through the storage and controlled discharge of excess water. When the scheme began the residents of 76 dwellings had to be relocated as well as the 'residents' of a cemetery. It is now popular for many water sports except swimming, which is dangerous, and is a reserve for wildfowl such as the greylag goose and whooper swan.

After about 3 km look for Dwyer's Brook, on your left. There is a monument here to a rebel scout called Dwyer. He was beheaded in 1798, but not before saving around 1,000 comrades also involved in the rebellion of that time. At Lackan detour right downhill to the Church of Our Lady of Mount Carmel. This little church was built in 1811 and is embellished with granite from nearby Ballyknockan. The views here are lovely. To the left are the rounded peaks of Black Hill, Moanbane and Silsean whose skirts fall to the lake's edge. Return to the main route and keep right at the school on leaving Lackan. This road leads to Ballyknockan about 5 km away. The road descends from Lackan and levels out near a bridge that you cross, over Ballynastockan Brook. Eventually you will arrive at the outskirts of Ballyknockan village. On the left is a picnic area with granite tables and seats. There is also a granite stone erected by the people of the village to a local man, Christy McEvoy. Ballyknockan is renowned for its granite and many of Dublin's famous buildings were built using this stone. As you pass through the village look for the mural, depicting a rural community, on the gable end of a house.

About 2 km from Ballyknockan is a T-junction. Close by at a brook is a sweathouse, a beehive-shaped structure. This was an Irish form of sauna. Fires of turf and wood were used to heat it. After sweating out their aches and pains the occupants would jump into the brook. Turn right at the T-junction onto the R758 for Valleymount. On your right, as you pass through the village, is St Joseph's Church, dated 1803. It is a most unusual design with wonderful stained-glass windows depicting religious images. Some say returning emigrants from Mexico influenced the architecture and, as with other buildings around these parts, Ballyknockan granite was used in the construction. After Valleymount you will cross a bridge. Continue on the R758 and watch for a turn to the right for the lakeshore. Detour here for a different perspective of the lake, right at the water's edge. Return to the R758.

After 2 km you will cross a bridge over the lake for the final time. Another 1 km will take you to a T-junction with the busy N81. Turn left here and cycle 1 km to the sign for Russborough House. Left at the sign will take you into Russborough Park, an amenity managed by the Electricity Supply Board (ESB), and a right turn onto a third-class road brings you to Russborough House. The entrance to this fine Palladian-style mansion is a few hundred metres on the left. It was built with Ballyknockan granite *c*. 1741 for Joseph Leeson, later Earl of Milltown. The architect was Richard Castle. The house is more recently famous for art robberies, one in 1974 by the IRA and a second in 1986 by Dublin criminals. Most of the paintings were recovered. Currently the house is undergoing major refurbishment. It is normally open during the summer months, although while work is ongoing its art collection has been removed. On leaving the Russborough grounds, turn left, continuing on the third-class road to a T-junction about 1 km away. Turn right and cycle for about 3 km to a roundabout, left at the roundabout will soon take you back into Blessington and a well-earned rest.

32. SALLY GAP SOUTH (WICKLOW)

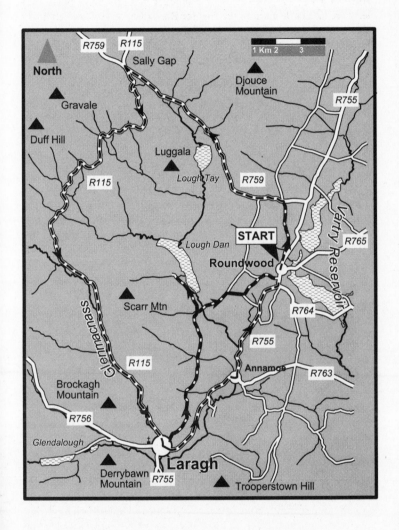

32. Sally Gap South (Wicklow)

Distance (km)	41–45
Cycling time (hours)	$4^1/_2$–5
Terrain	Mountainous
Roads (osi 56 map)	Mainly on quiet regional roads
Attractions	Lakes, Mountains, Rivers, Waterfall, Woodland, a little Heritage

Scenically this is one of the most spectacular routes and reveals Wicklow at its natural best. Rugged mountains plunging into gaping lakes, and rivers cascading along mountain valleys characterise the beautiful landscape. However, there is a price to pay, a few serious hills to climb and of course to descend.

The route begins at Roundwood and rises for about 240 m over 4 km. At this level there are breathtaking views over Lough Tay and Luggala Estate, owned by the Guinness family. The road then descends before gradually ascending again to the crossroads at Sally Gap. From here the route turns onto the Military Road where you reap your reward from the previous hard work. It descends from the bleak beauty of the Sally Gap into lush, evergreen forest. Once through the forest you can view the spectacular Glenmacnass Falls, and then follow the river of the same name back to Laragh. From Laragh you can choose an easy route or a more difficult but scenic one back to Roundwood. I would advise choosing a clear day to properly appreciate the scenery. Take food along with the obligatory drinks, as provisions are not obtainable during the cycle.

From Dublin, take the N11/M11 past Bray to Kilmacanoge. Leave the main road here following the signs for Roundwood on the R755. The village is about 40 km from the City. Park your car around the village centre.

Cycle back in the direction of Dublin to the outskirts of Roundwood, and turn left onto a minor road at the sign for Sally Gap. After 2 km there is a junction with the R759. Turn left continuing to follow the sign for Sally Gap, about 8 km away. The road begins to ascend quite steeply, about 240 m over 4 km, and unless you have very low gears you might like to dismount and walk on parts. Once you reach the top there is a forestry road to the right leading into the mixed conifer forest called Ballinastoe Wood. A path here forms part of the 130-km Wicklow Way walk that leads over Djouce Mountain to the northeast. In 1946 a French JU-52 3-engine airplane crash-landed during a storm on Djouce. The plane with a crew of 4 had been charted to fly 23 French girl guides to Ireland for a camping holiday. The occupants survived the crash although some were injured. Amazingly, too, the plane remained intact giving the survivors shelter during the storm until help eventually arrived.

To the left are magnificent views down to Lough Tay and the Luggala Estate. The Cloghoge River flows through the Estate into the northern part of the Lough. The river then continues from the southern part to Lough Dan further south. The mountain plunging into Lough Tay is Luggala or Fancy Mountain. The Luggala Estate itself is associated with the Guinness family and the imported white sandy beach at the head of the saucer-shaped Lough Tay could be likened to a pint of the black stuff the family are so famous for. The 4th Lord Oranmore and Browne married into the Guinness family. Tragically one of their sons Tara Browne was killed in a car accident in London. He was a friend of John Lennon and the tragic event is remembered in the Beatles song 'A Day in the Life'. Lord Oranmore and Browne himself is believed to hold the record as the longest-serving member of the British House of Lords, taking his seat in 1927 and losing it in 1999 under new government reforms of the House. He died in 2002 aged 100.

As you continue to Sally Gap, over 5 km away, the route descends quite steeply to Sheepbanks Bridge where the road veers to the left. After the bridge you pass through Ballinastoe Wood before finally breaking into open ground. Behind is a view of Lough Tay, ahead the ground is dressed in fern and gorse. The rising road in front meanders in the distance through stunning and desolate landscape to Sally Gap. When you see the roadside sign for Sally Gap you expect more. But all there is are crossroads and road signs and maybe a few sheep for company. At around 500 m above sea level this is highest climb of the Wicklow 200. This challenging, non-competitive cycle takes place over one day every June. It covers 200 km around the roads of County Wicklow and attracts over 1,000 cyclists each year from many countries. The shorter Wicklow Challenge takes place on the same day and shares most of the route with the Wicklow 200. The event is open to all cyclists and has been organised each year by the Irish Veteran Cyclists' Association since 1981.

From Sally Gap follow the sign to Laragh, 19 km away. This road is known as the Military Road (route 34), and was built by the English military to move men and supplies to suppress the rebels of 1798 still operating in the Wicklow Mountains. The road begins a descent and in the main descends all the way to Laragh. After about 6 km it passes through a forest of evergreens for about 3 km before breaking into open ground again. Not far away is a car park on the right, and just beyond is the Glenmacnass Waterfall. The water here tumbles 76 m into the great glacial valley of the Glenmacnass River, a fabulous sight particularly when there has been a lot of rainfall. The Glenmacnass River flows on the right near the road all the way to Laragh, about 8 km away. The road descends quite steeply and soon the first sign of settled civilisation appears in the form of houses. Gradually the numbers increase as you draw closer to Laragh, which by the way is within shouting distance of the ancient monastic settlement of Glendalough (route 36). In Laragh turn left onto the R755 in the direction of Annamoe and Roundwood.

From Laragh you have a choice of two routes back to Roundwood. You can take the 10-km, easier-but-less-spectacular route on the R755 via Annamoe. The alternative is a bit longer and much more challenging. However, it is a lot more scenic and takes in Lough Dan, a scenic area popular with scouts. For this route, turn left off the R755 at the sign for St John's Church, near the outskirts of the village. The road ascends quite steeply for the next few kilometres before descending again. About 4 km from Laragh you will converge with the Wicklow Way while ascending again towards Oldbridge, about 2 km further. Detour here at the sign for Lough Dan, about 3 km there and back; expect a stiff climb. Lough Dan is bigger than Lough Tay. It has 3 rivers to maintain it, the Inchavore and Cloghoge flowing in on the north side, and the Avonmore flowing out on the south.

Return to the main road and continue over the Avonmore River, through a deciduous forest and on to Roundwood, about 4 km away. There are a number of establishments in the village for you to rest and replenish before returning to your car. Most likely you will need it, especially if you take the alternative route.

33. ASHFORD–ROUNDWOOD (WICKLOW)

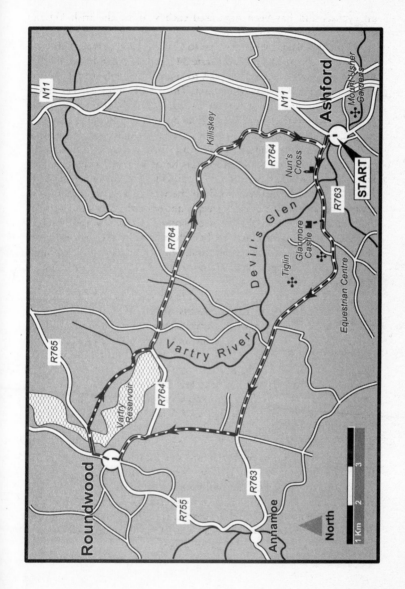

Distance (km)	28
Cycling time (hours)	$2^3/4$
Terrain	Mountainous
Roads (osi 56 map)	Three-quarters regional, remainder on third-class
Attractions	Lake, Mountains, River, Woodland, Gardens, a little Heritage

This picturesque route may suit the more robust cyclist, but those less vigorous can walk up the steeper hills and still enjoy its delights. It begins at Ashford and gets the hard hill climb out of the way first. This leaves the return journey an easy one, as it is mainly downhill. Ashford itself is a quaint village situated on the River Vartry. After leaving here the route begins to ascend steeply near the Devil's Glen, through which the Vartry flows. Having passed the Glen's wooded areas the landscape opens to stunning views whilst descending to the tranquillity of Roundwood. After Roundwood the going gets much easier, passing the Vartry Reservoir and through typical Wicklow garden country. Finally the route descends back into Ashford, where the nearby Mount Usher Gardens are a treat for the flora lover.

From Dublin take the N11, which in part becomes the M11, and pass Bray and Newtown Mount Kennedy to Ashford. Cross a roundabout to the town centre and park. Ashford is about 45 km from Dublin.

Once on your bike, return to the roundabout and turn left onto the R763. After a few hundred metres turn left again at a fork junction staying on the R763. A prominent hill comes into view to the left, this is Carrick Mountain. After 1 km you will come to Nun's Cross and the old church here on the right dates from 1817. Continue over the Vartry River, and nearby take the next right onto a minor road for Glanmore Castle. After passing through a pleasant wooded area turn right onto a track at a crossroads, and cycle up the hill to the castle. Glanmore Castle is actually a castellated country house built around 1804 for Francis Synge MP to designs by Francis Johnston. A famous son of the Synge family was John Millington Synge, co-founder of the Abbey Theatre. His controversial play, *Playboy of the Western World*, caused riots outside the Abbey in 1907 because of how its language and reference to the virtues of Irish women were perceived. Synge suffered from Hodgkin's disease and unfortunately died before his 38th birthday. Perhaps his greatest work was yet to come, but alas we will never know. On the day we were here Glanmore Castle was for sale.

From Glanmore Castle, go back on the track to the crossroads. If you are interested in horses turn right to visit the nearby Devil's Glen Holiday and Equestrian Centre. After, return to the crossroads and take the right fork. At the junction with the R763 turn right. Cycle to a Y-junction about 1 km further on. Keep right in the direction of Annamoe. The road ascends steeply for over 1 km before finally descending and opening up magnificent views of the Wicklow Hills to the left. The route passes through a wooded area before coming to the right turn for Tiglin, the National Mountain and White Water Centre. Tiglin offers a range of climbing, hillwalking and kayaking courses for the adventurous. After Tiglin the view opens to the right with the Vartry River flowing nearby. Continue past the right turn for Newtown Mount Kennedy. After 2.5 km, turn right at the staggered crossroads in the direction of Roundwood, about 3 km away. On this road there is a slight ascent, but the cycle is pleasant through broadleaved trees. After 2.5 km you come to a stop sign. Continue straight on following the sign for the Vartry Drive. The road levels out before finally descending into Roundwood. Roundwood claims to be the highest village in Ireland at 238 m above sea level. There was also much activity here during the rebellion of 1798 when General Joseph Holt of the United Irishmen led a successful campaign against the English army. He later emigrated to Australia where he died.

In Roundwood turn right at the junction with the church facing you onto the R755, in the direction of Bray. Cycle through town and then turn right onto the R764 at the sign for Newtown Mount Kennedy. Cross the Vartry Reservoir. The waterworks here supply parts of Dublin, North Wicklow and Dun Laoghaire, but not Roundwood itself. The waterworks were originally built in the 1860s by constructing an embankment across the valley of the Vartry River. A second reservoir was constructed above this one in 1923. Just after crossing the Vartry Reservoir turn right in the direction of Wicklow. On this road we observed that cattle on the right side of the road were lying down whereas those on the left side were standing up, strange indeed. After 2.5 km, some of which passes near the Reservoir, the road comes to a junction with the R764. Turn left towards Wicklow. After a few kilometres the road begins to descend and the sea can be seen in the distance on the left. Eventually it begins to level out as you approach Ashford. In Ashford you will come to a roundabout on the busy N11. Turn right here and pass over the Vartry River to the other side of town.

Here you will find Mount Usher Gardens on the left. Laid out along the banks of the River Vartry, Mount Usher was designed in the Robinsonian style. Trees, shrubs and herbaceous plants have been introduced from other parts of the world and planted in harmony with woodland and shade-loving plants. The extensive collection of rhododendrons, azaleas, magnolias and camellias is very colourful in spring. The gardens are open from March to October and an entry fee is required. If you fancy a snack there is a coffee shop, otherwise you could have one uptown before returning to your car.

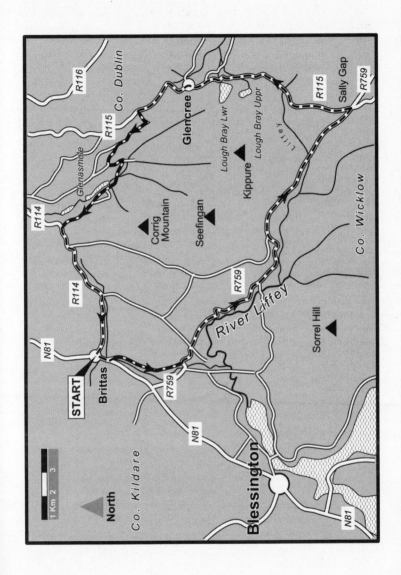

Distance (km)	45
Cycling time (hours)	$4^1/2$
Terrain	Mountainous
Roads (osi 50, 56 maps)	Three-quarters on regional, the remainder on third-class
Attractions	Lakes, Mountains, Rivers, Woodland, a little Heritage

This is quite a challenging route because of the combination of steep ascents and distance. But the range of scenery is well worth the effort and it is difficult to surpass the robust beauty of Sally Gap. As with all mountain runs you should choose a clear day to really appreciate the views. I would advise taking food with you as well as the obligatory drinks as watering holes are far apart.

The route begins at Brittas and gets you off the busy N81 quickly. It then heads across flat country towards Kilbride before turning onto the 'Braveheart' film trail where the River Liffey meanders nearby. After Cloghleagh Bridge the road begins to rise and the landscape changes from fertile farm to rough mountain. It rises to Sally Gap at around 500 m, a desolate crossroads where nature is both harsh and charming. From Sally Gap the road descends to Glencree by Upper and Lower Lough Bray. Passing by the delightful Glencree Valley, it then diverts onto a third-class road to Glenasmole Reservoir before varied gradients take you back to Brittas.

From the M50 take exit 11 for the N81. Follow the signs for Blessington staying on the N81. Brittas is about 22 km from the City. On entering the small village there is a pub on the right, park around here.

Once on your bicycle continue towards Blessington. About 1 km from Brittas fork left onto a third-class road at the sign for the South County Golf Club — just ahead is the Wicklow border. Soon after the noise of the N81 traffic fades and you will see the rounded hump of Woodend Hill ahead of you. At about 3.5 km from the N81 there is a junction with the R759 near Kilbride. Turn left in the direction of the sign for the Braveheart Drive and you will pass a pub. As you continue the River Liffey meanders into view on its way from Sally Gap, flowing in the opposite direction to you. You will pass over Cloghleagh Bridge about 2 km from the pub. Here the Shankill, a tributary of the Liffey, gushed energetically under the shade of broad-leaf trees, and just around the bend is a peaceful, old church and cemetery.

Continuing on, the landscape opens up and the loose stone-walls, so typical of parts of rural Ireland, become more conspicuous. Pass a junction with a signpost for Blessington and notice Sorrel Hill at 599 m to your right. Left is the less conspicuous Seefingan, even though it rises to 724 m. Excavations at a sandpit appear on the right and the Liffey meanders near the road again. Up to now the road has been fairly level but from here on to Sally Gap it ascends, quite steeply in places. Four km on is a bridge over the Liffey. It was near here that I came across 7 goats by the side of the road. Goats are not native to Ireland and were introduced for milk, meat and skin. However, over the years they have escaped captivity or were let loose and they thrive in remote and rocky areas. Initially these goats were as curious of me as I of them. After retreating a little from the road, the 7 horned heads gawked in my direction. Eventually they got bored with me fumbling with my camera and trotted up the mountainside without getting their picture taken.

A little less than 3 km from the bridge takes you to Sally Gap. The roads crossing here seem to disappear into infinity, giving an incredible feeling of remoteness. The raw beauty is inspiring and just northwest is the imposing Kippure Mountain whereabouts the Liffey rises. It is no wonder that several films were made in the area, among them 'Braveheart' and 'Dancing at Lughnasa'. At this stage you will have travelled 18 km from Brittas.

At the crossroads turn left onto the R115. Thankfully the road descends, a welcome respite after the long push up. After 5 km, take the time to view the corries, Lough Bray Upper and the larger Lough Bray Lower. The Lower Lough is more difficult to see from the road but there is a track to it. The R115 is also known as the Military Road. Construction commenced in 1800 and it ran from Rathfarnham in Dublin to Aghavannagh in Wicklow and it still does. You can imagine how difficult it must have been to cut a road through this disobliging terrain; in fact it took 9 years. However, the road allowed the Redcoats to bring in men and supplies to help put down the insurgents still in action after the 1798 Rebellion, and eventually they did. The route continues to descend to Glencree, just off the road about 7 km from Sally Gap. It is well worth stopping here to view the Glencree Valley (route 37) extending to your right and beyond, to the Great Sugar Loaf mountain with its conspicuous pimple-like peak. There is a large building in the village that was once a military barracks. Ironically it is now a Centre for Reconciliation, and has a coffee shop if you feel the need.

Once you continue the road ascends again. Take the second left turn, 2 km from Glencree, onto a third-class road. You will descend a steep hill to a dogleg, so take your time on the descent. In the distance is Glenasmole Reservoir stretching along the valley floor. The River Dodder flows into it before continuing to the City. Take the second turn left at the sign for Castlekelly and Glenasmole. At Castlekelly Bridge go sharp right in the direction of Glenasmole. After 1 km you will cross the River Dodder. The road then begins to ascend quite steeply with the reservoir on your right. At the end of the reservoir is a fine view over much of Dublin. Soon after you will come to a junction with the R114. Turn left here. There is another steep climb before eventually descending into Brittas and back to your car. The pub in Brittas serves food and you will probably need some.

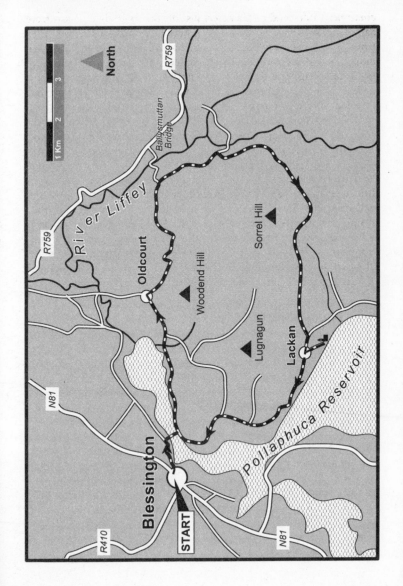

Distance (km)	25
Cycling time (hours)	2³/4
Terrain	Some mountainous
Roads (OSI 56 map)	All third-class
Attractions	Lake, Mountains, Woodland, some Heritage

Although this route is classified as mountainous there is only 4 km of challenging cycling. In the main, the rest is gradual ascent or steep descent. It is a beautiful route with remarkable mountain and lake scenery and for the most part is less busy than the more popular Lake Drive. It begins at Blessington, and crossing the scenic Blessington Bridge follows the northern shore of Poulaphouca Reservoir. This section is quite level, passing through deciduous wood seasonally filled with birdsong. As the road veers away from the lake, it ascends, gradually revealing fine views of the hills and forests to the north. The steep ascent up Sorrel Hill begins through coniferous wood, but the landscape becomes more barren with height. The descent is also steep and your brakes will be well exercised. Here the largest tract of Poulaphouca's water is in full view and remains so back to Blessington.

From the M50 take exit 11 for the N81. Follow the signs for Blessington staying on the N81. The town is about 28 km from the City. You can park in the town centre by the monument to the Marquis of Downshire. There are a number of inscriptions on it praising members of the family. I guess you could say that these old landlords were far from modest. St Mary's Church opposite dates from *c.* 1669.

Once on your bike, cycle past the hotel nearby and turn left at the sign for Lackan. Soon after the shallow arches of Blessington Bridge come into view. Descend to the bridge through a wooded area. Turn right over the bridge and left past a car park and picnic area. The waters of Poulaphouca Reservoir, also called the Blessington Lakes, are on your left. At about 4 km from Blessington you will pass over a small bridge called Woodend Bridge. Here you will leave the lake in the shadow of Woodend Hill. After a further 1 km take a right turn at a sign for Sally Gap and begin to ascend. A further 1 km will take you over Stoneyford Bridge and into an area of Ballys: Ballynasculloge,

Ballynattona, Ballysmuttan, Ballyward, Ballylow etc. Continue to climb and enjoy the views of the hills on your left. The fields are an amazing patchwork of different shapes together with a surface texture of trees, shrubs and open ground. On your right are coniferous woods. In contrast there is also bog in parts consisting of mosses and sedge.

Soon you will come to a junction, go right, away from the direction to Sally Gap. At the next junction keep right of the cul-de-sac and prepare for a steep ascent, 180 m over 3 km. This is Sorrel Hill. However, it is very pleasant to stop for a rest and step into the coniferous forest and listen. Silence prevails, broken only by the occasional calling bird or other shuffling creature. But with height the landscape changes to more barren ground where heather and wiry grass dominate; a place for sheep, and there were plenty. You have reached the highest point when you see a car park on your left. Sorrel Hill rises another 150 m to your right. In the opposite direction looking southeasterly is Mullaghcleevaun, at 849 m second only to Lugnaquilla as the highest mountain in the Wicklow range.

There is a rapid descent from the car park to the village of Lackan, so take it easy. The larger tract of the Poulaphouca Reservoir is in view all the way down, back to Blessington in fact. It is a magnificent sight. Lackan is a quaint village overlooking the reservoir. A movie called 'Widows Peak', and starring Mia Farrow, was made here in 1992. It is a comedy set in rural Ireland in the 1920s in a village ruled by women, mostly widows. I can imagine the set here being quite suitable. On entering Lackan turn right for Blessington, about 6 km away. Take a slight detour left at the sign for Our Lady of Mount Carmel Church. There are lovely views over the lake from the church, inaugurated in 1811. Return to the main road.

Continue to Blessington Bridge by the ridge of Lugnagun on your right. While passing these last few kilometres on your bicycle, consider another form of transport used in Blessington. A steam tram service ran from Blessington to Terenure in Dublin — the Dublin & Blessington Steam Tramway began operations in 1888. It took about an hour and a half for the 26-km journey, slower than a bicycle. No wonder the development of road transport led to its closure in 1932.

Cross the bridge once more; then turn left to Blessington and back to your car.

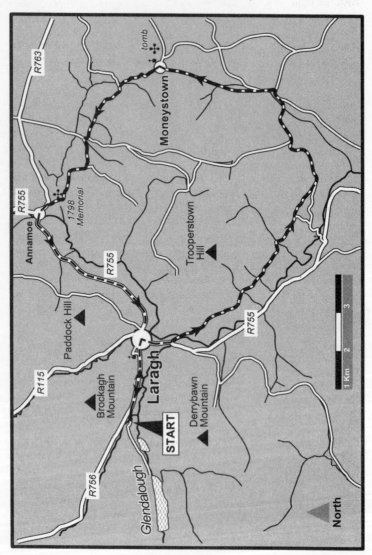

R763

tomb

Moneystown

R755

Annamoe

1798 Memorial

R755

Trooperstown Hill

R755

Paddock Hill

R115

Laragh

Brockagh Mountain

START

Derrybawn Mountain

R756

Glendalough

1 Km 2 3

North

Distance (km)	28
Cycling time (hours)	$3^1/2$
Terrain	Hilly
Roads (OSI 56 map)	Third-class except for about 8 km on regional
Attractions	Mountains, Woodland, Fishing, Heritage

For the most part this route follows quiet back roads, passing by Wicklow sheep grazing contentedly. Although it goes around the 430-m-high Trooperstown Hill, the terrain is hilly rather than mountainous. And of course there is the hallowed atmosphere and magnificent beauty of Glendalough.

The route begins at St Kevin's monastic site at Glendalough and then turns off the regional road soon after Laragh. The road ascends but the climb is not too taxing, and the scenery is rather pleasant under the shadow of Trooperstown Hill. It then passes through mainly pine forest before descending to Garryduff Crossroads. Then it's on to Moneystown where you can view some ancient standing stones and wonder about their origin. From here the route meanders back to Annamoe and, if you feel like it, a spot of fishing. Here the route joins a regional road to take you to Laragh with Trooperstown Hill in full view to your left. Finally pass through Laragh to Glendalough and enjoy the beauty and history of this unique place.

From Dublin, take the N11/M11 past Bray to Kilmacanoge. Leave the main road here following the signs for Glendalough, about 50 km from the City. There are two main car parks at Glendalough, one at the Visitor Centre and one at the Upper Lake. If you prefer to avoid the crowds at Glendalough you could always park at Laragh, 2 km before.

Cycle back to Laragh and turn right onto the R755 in the direction of Rathdrum. After 0.5 km and having passed a number of B&Bs, fork left onto a third-class road. Soon after, you will pass over the Avonmore River. Close by, it unites with the Glendasan River and nearer Laragh the Avonmore and Glenmacnass Rivers confluence. The road ascends in the shadow of Trooperstown Hill into a pine-forested area. Below is the Avonmore River, partially hidden in the valley.

Having cleared the forest you can view Kirikee Mountain to the right. About 9 km from Laragh is Garryduff Crossroads, turn left here. Trooperstown Hill is to the left, its peak partially hidden by a ridge. Keep left on the Y-junction immediately after Garryduff Crossroads. We took this route in May and the countryside was awash with wild gorse, its yellow flower a nice contrast to the green grasses and shrubbery.

About 3 km from Garryduff Crossroads is Moneystown. Detour right here at the church for about 100 m to see two small standing stones in a field on the left. Standing stones are ancient upright markers. Some marked burial sites or had a sacred role. Others may have had astronomical significance. Whatever their origin, positioning these substantial masses was a significant engineering achievement by our ancestors. However, the standing stones here are quite small in contrast to others about the country.

Return to the main road and continue in the direction of Roundwood. The road descends out of Moneystown and ahead the fields are set like a patchwork quilt on the hill side. The farms are mainly sheep for which Wicklow is famous, and occasionally the sheep take flight as you pass by. About 3 km from Moneystown is Moneystown Bridge, and the tall mountain in front is Scarr. Immediately after crossing this small bridge turn left, and after 1 km keep right. Follow the road and after another 1 km you will see an old entrance to an estate on the left. A local told me that this property belongs to the film star Daniel Day Lewis. Amongst the many parts he played was the challenging one of Christy Brown, the disabled artist from Dublin. Soon after is a bridge over a stream and a memorial to Andrew Thomas (1776–1800) who fought in the 1798 Rebellion alongside Michael Dwyer, the leader of a band of insurgents who held out against the British in these mountains for 5 years.

Continue on to the junction with the R763 and turn left into Annamoe. At a stop sign with the R755 go left in the direction of Laragh. Cross over the Avonmore River once again, and on the right is a trout farm. You can hire rod and bait and do a spot of fishing if the urge takes you. Continue towards Laragh on the R755. This is a busy road carrying the main tourist traffic to Glendalough but is very pleasant. The road is wooded on both sides and Trooperstown Hill can be viewed to the left. The road descends into Laragh, one of the busiest villages in Ireland, and a place where tourists and hillwalkers meet and greet in local hostelries. Continue through Laragh onto the R756 for Glendalough, 2 km away. On the way into Glendalough, look out for the parish church of St Kevin and detour to the right a little. This famine church was built during the Great Famine of the 1840s and has been restored since. The serene Meditation Garden here is designed to provide a place where nature, scripture and the history of Glendalough are combined in harmony.

Glendalough bustles with tourists and hillwalkers. It is indeed a magnificent place steeped in monastic history and natural beauty. Although bustling now it must have been a very lonely place when in the 6th century St Kevin, a hermit, came to live here. It is said he first lived in a tree on the north side of the Upper Lake, and then in a cave on the south side accessible by boat only. Later when his followers gathered in numbers, he founded a great monastery which lasted 6 centuries and became the monastic capital of Europe. However, like many others throughout Ireland, it suffered from Norse plundering. One of the most noted abbots in the 12th century was St Laurence O'Toole who afterwards became Archbishop of Dublin. You could spend a day here exploring the ruins of 7 churches and the ancient round tower, and take some walks to view the magnificent scenery. The Visitor Centre runs guided tours, exhibitions and audiovisual shows; there is an entry fee. The nearby hotel can provide you with refreshments before returning to your car and setting off for home.

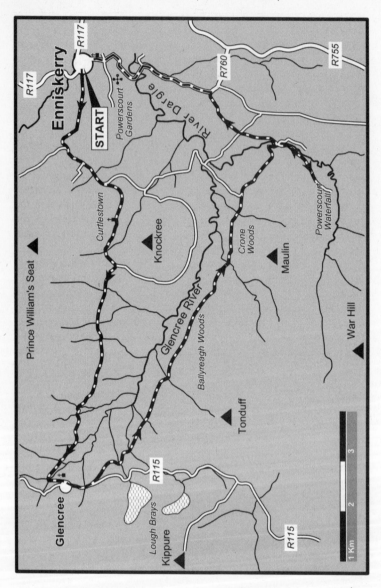

Distance (km)	28
Cycling time (hours)	$3^1/4$
Terrain	Mountainous
Roads (osi 56 map)	Mostly third-class
Attractions	Mountains, Woodland, Rivers, Waterfall, Gardens, Heritage

This is a delightfully scenic route circling the beautiful Glencree Valley from Enniskerry. Enniskerry itself is regarded as the gate to the Garden of Ireland. The town can be busy especially at weekends as people congregate before heading off for their selected activities. Generally the route ascends along the north side of the valley to the rural setting at Glencree. It then descends back to Enniskerry on the south side of the valley in the shadow of Tonduff and Maulin Mountains.

Expect a steep ascent out of Enniskerry, but then the climb becomes more gradual. From Glencree there is a superb view along the valley to the Great Sugar Loaf Mountain, unmistakable for its pimple-like peak. The return is mainly downhill before passing Powerscourt Waterfall, Ireland's highest, and then Powerscourt Gardens, claimed to be one of the world's greatest. There is also the magnificent 18th-century, Palladian-style mansion there. At this point you are almost back at Enniskerry and well-deserved replenishment.

Take the N11 from the City, which becomes the M11 for a bit, and exit at the sign for Enniskerry. Follow the signs eventually taking the R117 into Enniskerry, about 24 km from the City. As you approach the centre of the village there is a car park to your right. Turn right over the small bridge to it.

As you cycle out of the car park turn right back over the bridge to the clock tower in the village centre. Turn right again following the sign for the Glencree Drive. There is a steep gradient out of Enniskerry, about 60 m over 1 km. Eventually the road levels out and the climb becomes much easier. About 4 km from Enniskerry is Curtlestown. St Patrick's Church will be on the right, built in 1891. After passing the signs for the Wicklow Way you will come to Cloon Wood, mainly an oak forest with gorse and bracken ground-cover. Across the valley from Cloon are the rounded peaks of Tonduff, with War Hill and Djouce, rising to 725 m, in the background. The road into Glencree rises again and eventually turns in a dogleg through the small village. The large building here was originally built as a barracks to guard the northern end of the Military Road (route 34), which runs through to Glendalough. The building is now used as a Centre of Reconciliation to promote understanding amongst peoples of different backgrounds. There is an information centre and coffee shop as well. Having passed through Glencree, stop to view the magnificent scene along the valley to the Great Sugar Loaf, unmistakable for its great, big, pimply peak. On the right at the valley's edge are the rounded peaks of Tonduff and Maulin and on your left, Knocknagun and Prince William's Seat. The Glencree River runs through the centre of the valley. You will have crossed it as a stream whilst passing through Glencree.

Just past Glencree is a yield sign for the Military Road (R115). Join it for 100 m or so and then fork left onto a third-class road following the sign for the Glencree Drive. Immediately you begin to descend with the Great Sugar Loaf remaining in front of you. In winter, in particular, this part of the route is shaded from the sun and the descent can be chilly. About 7 km from Glencree is Crone Wood. Originally one of oak trees, the great trees were felled over the centuries for shipbuilding and house building. It is now planted with conifers mainly. This area became a hideout following the 1798 Rebellion for groups of insurgents who continued to harass the English militia. Continue another 2 km to the S-bend that crosses the Dargle River on Waterfall Bridge. I saw a grey squirrel bound across a ditch here. Apparently this mammal was introduced from North America and is now widespread. It can be a pest to those growing forests commercially.

Just past the bridge on the right is Powerscourt Waterfall. It is the highest in Ireland where the River Dargle plunges 130 m, and is particularly dynamic after rain. There is a nature trail around the waterfall, and an entrance fee to see both. On continuing you will ascend for about 1 km passing a crossroads. Another 1 km will take you to the R760. Turn left here for Powerscourt Gardens. It takes you through a wooded area and across the narrow Tinnehinch Bridge over the River Dargle. After another hill climb you will come to Powerscourt Demesne on your left. Another 1 km cycle will bring you to the house through very pleasant grounds and past a golf course. This magnificent mansion replaced a castle built by the Anglo-Norman de la Poer. The mansion itself was badly damaged by fire in 1974 and has since been rebuilt. The gardens consist of 47 acres and include Italian and Japanese gardens. An entrance fee will be required.

On leaving Powerscourt turn left into Enniskerry and pass the clock tower on your left. It was showing the wrong time on the day I was there. Just before you cross the bridge to the car park there is a small seating area on the right. Here you will find a plaque remembering local man Charles Keegan, the first Irishman to win a World Ploughing Contest in Austria. As you load your car listen for the babble of the small Cookstown River nearby.

38. Ballykissangel (Wicklow)

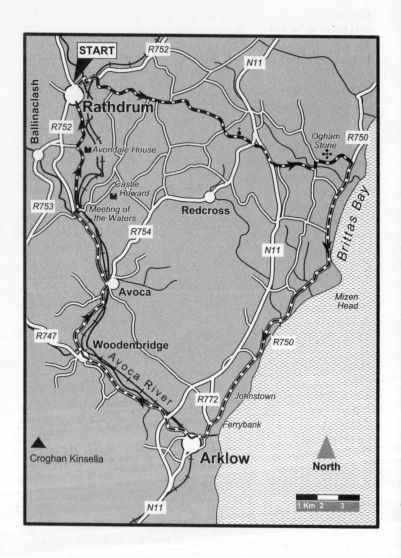

Distance (km)	56
Cycling time (hours)	6
Terrain	Hilly
Roads (OSI 62 map)	Half on regional, remainder on third-class except for 1 km on N11
Attractions	Mountains, Glen, River, Woodland, Coast, Heritage

This is a very lovely cycle passing through the Vale of Avoca immortalised in Moore's melody 'The Meeting of the Waters'. It also takes in the village of Avoca, itself famous for the TV series 'Ballykissangel'. The route is a little testing inland because of the hills but none the less is well worth the effort.

It begins at Rathdrum and heads for the coast to Brittas Bay and some of the finest beaches on the east coast. The route hugs the shoreline to Arklow once famous for shipbuilding and where the Avoca River meets the sea. It then turns inland following the river through the Vale of Avoca to Woodenbridge, whose wooden bridge, from which the village got its name, disappeared c. 1770. The route continues through the Vale to pretty Avoca, and it's no wonder it was chosen for the fictitious 'Ballykissangel'. The village is also as easy-going as the TV series. On the way back to Rathdrum visit Avondale House and Forest Park, once home to one of Ireland's great political leaders Charles Stewart Parnell.

From Dublin City, take the N11/M11 past Ashford to Rathnew. At Rathnew take the R752 to Rathdrum via Glenealy. Rathdrum is about 59 km from the City. You should find parking without having to drive into the town centre.

Once on your bicycle go back on the R752 climbing a steep hill to a right turn, about 1.5 km from the town. Take this right turn in the direction of a sign for Ballindoyle Farmhouse. The road continues to rise 100 m for about 4 km. On descent there are nice views towards the coast on the left. Continue on the road following signs for the N52 and Redcross. After a further 3.5 km you will come to a church. Pass the church and cross the R754 in the direction of Brittas Bay, 6 km away. Soon you will come to the busy N11. Turn right onto it and cycle for about 1 km to a left turn. Take the left turn onto a minor road and soon after go left again at a Y-junction. Two kilometres from the N11 is a T-junction beside which there is a small equestrian centre. Turn left, passing the equestrian centre. Cycle past a nearby cemetery with the remains of an old church inside. Soon after is a yield sign at a junction. Turn right and about 100 m further at the roadside is an ogham stone. Ogham, commonly pronounced oh-am, is an alphabet of 25 characters that was used to inscribe wood and stone in Celtic times. Basically ogham characters consist of combinations of perpendicular or angled strokes meeting or crossing a centre line. Note the lines marked into the stone here and fair play to you if you can interpret them.

Continue towards the coast and the R750, about 2 km away. At the junction with the R750, turn right onto it. Cycle for about 2 km and arrive at the signboard for Brittas Bay. Soon after is a car park on the left. Going left here will take you to the fine sandy beach enclosed by dunes, known as the North Beach. Looking south from the beach is Mizen Head, a point used for weather forecasting. Return to the R750 and continue cycling towards Mizen Head, about 3 km. Look for the wind generators located 13 km out to sea. These are installed on the Arklow Bank, sand banks which were given a wide berth by marine craft well before the wind generators were put there. Now the tall structures provide a fine beacon as well as power, and smaller craft usually sail on the landside of the generators. Near Mizen Head the road veers away from the coast but returns after 3 km, and Arklow, about 8 km away, comes into view. It must be said that the road here is rather like a third-class road instead of the regional type it is. But thankfully the traffic is very light, or at least it was on the day we passed.

Eventually you reach the outskirts of Arklow. Cycle on to a yield sign and turn left. Cross the 19-arches bridge, built *c.* 1759, over the Avoca River and turn right uptown to a monument to Father Michael Murphy, a leader and hero of the rebellion of 1798. However, he lost his life at the Battle of Arklow and his death was a severe blow to morale. The rout of the United Irishmen in Arklow put an end to their advance north and forced them back to Wexford, and final defeat. Arklow has a great shipbuilding tradition and was famous for some of Ireland's finest small boats. The celebrated transatlantic yachtsman Sir Francis Chicester Clarke had his yacht *Gypsy Moth* II built here.

Continue on to a small roundabout and turn right in the direction of Avoca on the R747. Cycle through the first part of the Vale of Avoca to Woodenbridge, about 7 km from Arklow. The area around Woodenbridge is associated with goldmining when in 1785 the finding of a nugget weighing a quarter of an ounce led to a gold rush. The Woodenbridge Hotel claims to be one of Ireland's oldest dating back to 1608. There is a fine golf course before it now. Keep right at the hotel, onto the R752, in the direction of Avoca. As you cycle, you will see evidence of mining on the hillsides and the stacks built for the old mining steam engines. Copper and brimstone were produced from the valley; however, all mining ceased in the early 1980s. After 3 km you come to Avoca village. You will need to detour right for the village centre. Avoca is noted for its tweeds and more recently for the TV production, 'Ballykissangel', a laid-back and somewhat comical view of rural life in Ireland.

Return to the R752 and continue for about 3.5 km to the Meeting of the Waters. Thomas Moore immortalised the Vale of Avoca when, at this place in 1807, he wrote his famous melody 'The Meeting of the Waters'. Here the waters of the Avonmore and Avonbeg Rivers confluence. It is indeed a beautiful place as espoused by Moore, 'There is not in the wide world a valley so sweet as that vale in whose bosom the bright waters meet.' Just past the Meeting of the Waters is a right turn onto a third-class road off the R752. Take it and soon after turn left. Watch for Castle Howard set amongst the trees to your right behind you. Originally built as a fortified house for the early mining bosses around the 17th century, it was later sold to Robert Howard, a brother of the Viscount of Wicklow. The castle has had many famous visitors including Thomas Moore and Walter Scott. Modern owners have included Herman Linders, best known for composing the music for Queen Elizabeth II's coronation. Castle Howard is on private grounds.

From the R752 the terrain rises steeply for about 0.5 km and then rises gradually to 140 m above sea level before descending to a yield sign, about 3 km from the R752. Turn right here in the direction of Avondale House less than 1 km away. Avondale House was built *c.* 1777 in the Georgian style. It was the birthplace and home of Charles Stewart Parnell (1846–1891), one of the greatest political leaders in Irish history. The house is set in a forest park of over 500 acres with tree trails and walks. The house and park are open to visitors. Return

175

to the main road and continue. The road rises slightly before descending into Rathdrum, about 2 km away. At the yield sign cycle directly across into the town and back to your car or have a snack in one of the local watering holes. While doing so think on a great battle that took place here in 1599 when Sir Henry Harrington's forces were beaten by the local O'Toole and O'Byrne clans. Sir Henry had come especially to put manners on the clans, but he misjudged them and his men ran for their lives, tails tucked tightly between their legs.

39. Glenmalure and Aughrim (Wicklow)

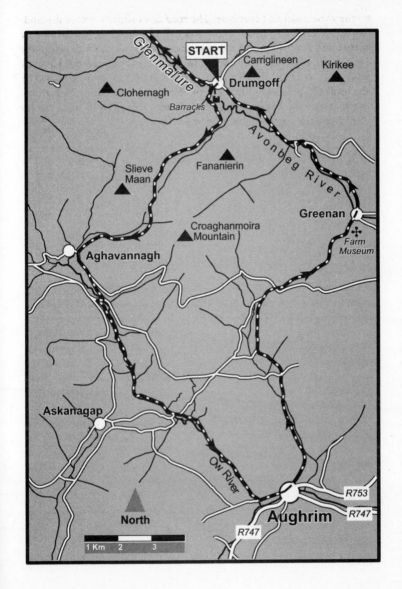

START

Carriglineen

Kirikee

Glenmalure

Drumgoff

Clohernagh

Barracks

Avonbeg River

Slieve Maan

Fananierin

Croaghanmoira Mountain

Greenan

Farm Museum

Aghavannagh

Askanagap

Ow River

Aughrim

R753

R747

R747

North

1 Km   2   3

Distance (km)	45
Time (hours)	4¹/₂
Terrain	Mountainous
Roads (osi 56, 62 maps)	Mainly third-class
Attractions	Mountains, Glen, Rivers, Fishing, Woodland, some Heritage

This is a challenging cycle, but surely to include the most spectacular glen in County Wicklow is worth it. Glenmalure is outstanding for many reasons. The towering peak of Lugnaquilla, rising to the south-west, is one of the highest mountains in Ireland. The Avonbeg River, flowing majestically beneath deciduous and coniferous forests, washes its floor, and the great granite boulders there provided hiding for the rebels that once harried the Crown. And besides, there is much more to offer on this very scenic route.

The cycling begins at Drumgoff and takes the spur through Glenmalure. After, the route returns to Drumgoff and then heads on a tough climb on the Military Road towards Aghavannagh. However, the views make the effort well worth the hard work. After the descent towards Aughrim, the landscape changes to a pleasant wooded one, before arriving in this picturesque village. From Aughrim the scenery becomes a little less spectacular, but picks up again as the route passes through towering peaks on the return to Drumgoff.

From Dublin, take the N11/M11 past Bray to Kilmacanoge. Leave the main road here following the signs for Glendalough. Drive to Laragh, a village about 2 km before Glendalough, and turn left onto the R755 in the direction of Rathdrum. After 2 km, turn right following the sign for Glenmalure. After another 9 km, you will come to a crossroads, turn left and immediately you will see the Glenmalure Lodge Hotel on the left. There is a car park opposite. This area is called Drumgoff and is about 57 km from Dublin.

Once on your bicycle, cycle back to the crossroads and continue straight across onto the road with the cul-de-sac sign, the road continues for 6 km. Soon after, you come upon an inscribed boulder commemorating Fiach McHugh O'Byrne (1580) and Michael Dwyer

(1798). The dates refer to two battles that were fought in the tranquil setting of Glenmalure. In 1580, the O'Byrne clan ambushed a column of 1,000 soldiers led by Lord Grey de Wilton, the Lord Deputy. The battle was short-lived, but over 800 lives were lost, a terrible defeat for the English. The leader of the O'Byrnes, Fiach McHugh, was eventually beheaded in 1597 and his head impaled on the gates of Dublin Castle as a deterrent to others — nasty.

In 1798, General Eustace and about 80 Redcoats were on patrol in Glenmalure. They were ambushed by rebels led by Michael Dwyer and forced to retreat as they were outnumbered. The rebels pursued them for several miles constantly sniping at the troops. The following day Eustace returned with 500 soldiers. However, Dwyer and his men had retreated into the mountains from where they harried the Redcoats for many years after. Eventually Michael Dwyer surrendered in 1805, and was transported to penal servitude in Australia. He later became a constable near Sydney. He remained in Australia, and died in 1825.

Continue cycling through the Glen, the Avonbeg River flows to your left. The towering Lugnaquilla, at 925 m, is also to your left. Ahead is the somewhat lower Camenabologue, Table Mountain and Conavalla, and to the right Mullacor and Lugduff Mountains. After about 3 km you will come to a disused lead mine at Ballinafunshoge. It was operated by the Royal Irish Mining Company in the early 19th century, and workers were accommodated in the nearby Drumgoff Barracks. Another 3 km will take you to the end of the road at a bridge over the Avonbeg. The road then becomes a track used by hillwalkers. There is also a car park here.

Return to Drumgoff. At the crossroads turn right onto the Military Road and over the Avonbeg in the direction of Aughrim. On the left is the imposing Drumgoff Barracks. This, along with a series of barracks, was built by the militia on the Military Road to store men and equipment in the campaign against the 1798 rebels. It later housed miners from the Ballinafunshoge lead mine. Today it is a ruin. Soon after the road climbs steeply, about 300 m over 5 km, and you can expect a challenging cycle. The road rises above the lush vegetation of Glenmalure to the more barren ground, typical of the Wicklow Mountains. At the side of the road was an abundance of foxglove, a wild flower with pinkish-purple, bell-like flowers. At the top is a track leading into a forest; you could take a well-earned rest here if it's not too windy.

Now the descent starts and you could build up a right head of steam without trying over the next few kilometres. So keep those brakes exercised. As the hill eases off, watch for the turn to the left onto a minor road at Aghavannagh. Once on this road for 1 km you will come to a fork, keep right. Turn right again at the next junction after another km. You will now cross over the Ow River, and soon after is a junction with the road to Aughrim, turn left onto this main road. The cycling here is pleasant through wooded country, with the Ow gurgling nearby on the left. After 1 km you will cross over the river and the road continues through lush green ferns and trees. Follow the road for about 7 km into Aughrim. This picturesque village has a small lake where fishing is available at a charge. A local 1798 heroine was Anne Devlin. She was a niece of Michael Dwyer and got involved in the rebellion by carrying messages. Later she was associated with Robert Emmet, leader of the botched rising of 1803. She was arrested after the rising and spent almost 3 years in prison, often in solitary confinement. Eventually she was released, and lived until 1851 when she died in extreme poverty.

In the centre of the village turn left at the memorial for 1798 back into the country. The patchwork fields here are in contrast to the bareness of the mountain landscape earlier. After 4 km you come to Macreddin, and just before the village the road begins to climb quite steeply. Cycle for 3 km to a crossroads and go straight through, following the sign for Glenmalure, about 10 km away. After the crossroads the road begins to descend to Greenan, 3 km. On the way in is the Greenan Farm Museum and Maze. In Greenan, cross the Avonbeg River and at a yield sign turn left for Glenmalure. As you approach within a few kilometres of Glenmalure, the mountains get closer. You will pass through Kirikee overshadowed by a mountain of the same name. Finally you arrive back in Drumgoff, and are well deserved of a treat. You can have one in the Glenmalure Lodge, which, by the way, was built in the early 19th century and used as a hunting lodge by the Earl of Meath. I'm not sure whether game will be on the menu though.

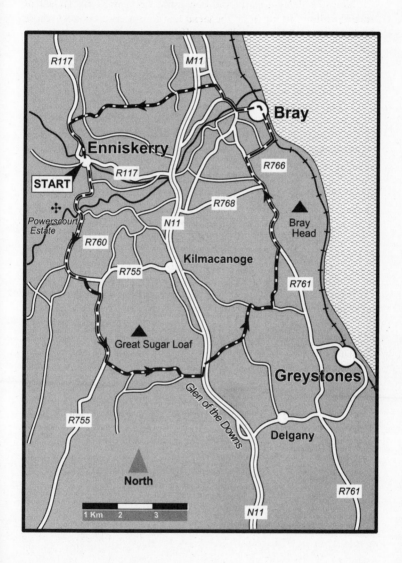

40. The Sugar Loafs (Wicklow, Dublin)

Distance (km)	30
Cycling time (hours)	$4^1/2$
Terrain	Mountainous
Roads (OSI 56 map)	Half regional and half third-class
Attractions	Mountains, Woodland, Garden, Coast, Heritage

This is a grand mix of coast and mountain landscape which offers a bit of a challenge on a most scenic route. The terrain climbs from sea level to 280 m around the majestic peaks of the Great Sugar Loaf and Little Sugar Loaf Mountains.

The route begins in the timeless town of Enniskerry which was and still is influenced by the great Powerscourt Estate nearby. It climbs out of the village to the Estate and continues south and east of the Great Sugar Loaf. The route then descends offering lovely views of the sea, and after passing over the N11 it climbs by the Little Sugar Loaf on the way to the old Victorian town of Bray. This once-famous holiday resort still retains an aura of candy floss and icecream as cheery folk perambulate the promenade. From Bray the route turns west back towards Enniskerry and a final glimpse of the imposing Sugar Loafs, before returning to your car and a soak in the atmosphere of the village.

Take the N11 from the City, which becomes the M11 for a bit. Near Bray, exit at the sign for Enniskerry. Follow the signs, eventually taking the R117, to the village. It is about 24 km from the City. Near the centre is a car park on the right as you drive in. Turn right over the bridge, spanning the Cookstown River, and park your car.

Once on your bicycle take the R760 in the direction of Roundwood. Expect a steep climb to the Powerscourt Estate, about 1 km out of town. The estate consists of a magnificent 18th-century Palladian-style mansion within which is a shopping area and terrace café. The gardens are said to be world-famous with over 200 varieties of trees and shrubs. Generally the place is very busy with tourists, especially during the summer months. But there are lovely views as you cycle the avenue towards the house, with the pimply peak of the Great Sugar Loaf dominating the left. There is an entry fee to the house and gardens but certain areas are accessible for free.

182

40. The Sugar Loafs (Wicklow, Dublin)

After visiting Powerscourt, return to the main road and turn right to continue. Having passed a golf course on the left, the road descends to Tinnehinch Bridge over the Dargle River. Continue on the main road following the sign for Roundwood. Pass the turn for Powerscourt Waterfall, this is about 3 km from Enniskerry. Then take the second right, after descending 1 km, onto a third-class road. Here there is a short but steep climb to the junction with the busy R755. Turn right onto it and expect another steep incline for 2 km. At the top, turn left onto a third-class road. Here the road is more level and quiet of traffic. The landscape is rather barren with the Great Sugar Loaf keeping company to your left as you cycle along. After about 1 km the coast comes into view and you start to descend steeply. Keep your fingers at the brake levers to control your descent. Finally after about 1.5 km you come to a junction, turn left. Once you reach the N11 cross the bridge over the dual carriageway and take the turn left. Continue straight on to a stop sign at a T-junction, about 3 km from the N11; turn left again. This is a pleasant cycle through a wooded area with the Little Sugar Loaf to your left.

After cycling about 1.5 km you come to a junction with the R761, turn left for Bray. As you cycle into Bray you will see ahead the distant red and white stacks of Poolbeg Power Station in Dublin City. You come to a roundabout after 2 km, cycle straight across. Continue through the next roundabout and through traffic lights which lead to a cycling lane. At the next traffic lights turn right following the sign for the seafront, on your right-hand side will be Bray Head. Continue to the seafront. The road along the seafront is one way. However, you can dismount and stroll along the wide promenade towards the harbour soaking up the atmosphere, particularly on a fine day. Up to 1854 Bray was quite an insignificant fishing village. But the arrival of the railway combined with the Victorian fondness for seawater transformed the town into a fashionable holiday resort. Hotels and villas were built along the seafront and attracted many who wished to benefit from the sea air and water. Imagine the top hats tipped to rustling petticoats as Victorian ladies and gents passed each other while perambulating the promenade. At the back of the harbour we found a large number of mute swans who vented their anger on a lone dog swimming after a stick. The dog bravely retrieved the stick and sensibly made a hasty retreat, as a few of the birds raised their wings and hissed threateningly.

40. The Sugar Loafs (Wicklow, Dublin)

From the harbour cycle 0.5 km inland, under the railway bridge, to the junction with the R761; turn right onto this main road over the Dargle River. Cycle for a little less than 1 km and turn left onto Old Connaught Avenue. Around this point you cross the border into County Dublin. Soon after, you pass over the M11 motorway. After 0.5 km turn left following the sign for Enniskerry, and immediately right continuing to follow the signs for the village, 4 km away. The road begins to climb quite steeply, but to your left are fine views of the two Sugar Loafs. Finally you cross back into County Wicklow before coming to a yield sign. At the sign, turn left back into Enniskerry and to your car. Take a look at the clock tower in the centre of the village. It was built by the son of the 5th Viscount Powerscourt in honour of his father. The giant timepiece gives the town a unique character, and what's more a pleasant coffee shop sits in its shadow.

A. Routes by County

No.	Name	County	Distance (km)	Time (hours)	Terrain	Roads	OSI Maps	Attractions
1	Fairy Castle Pub Crawl	Dublin	20	2½	Mountainous	Two-thirds on regional, the remaining on third-class. Busy stretch around Marlay Park. Route can be busy on weekends and holidays	50	Mountains, Woodland, a little Heritage, Old pubs
2	Brian Boru Circuit	Dublin, Fingal	44	5	Hilly (in part)	Three-quarters on cycle track, remainder on a mix of regional and third-class	50	Coast, Park, Wildlife sanctuary, Heritage
34	Sally Gap North	Dublin, Wicklow	45	4½	Mountainous	Three-quarters on regional, remainder on third-class	50, 56	Lakes, Mountains, Rivers, Woodland, a little Heritage
4	Fair Fingal	Fingal	30	2½	Rolling (mainly)	Half third-class and half regional	43	Coast, Gardens, Windmills, Heritage
5	Lambay Views	Fingal	25	2½	Hilly (verging on)	Two-thirds on third-class, the remainder on regional	43	Coastal views, Bird-watching, some Heritage
7	Bachall Iosa	Fingal	37	4	Hilly	All on regional except for 4 km on third-class	43	Rolling countryside, Music, Heritage
8	The Estuary Circuit	Fingal	50	5¼	Flat	Half regional and half third-class	43, 50	Coast, Park, Bird-watching, Heritage

A. Routes by County

No.	Name	County	Distance (km)	Time (hours)	Terrain	Roads	OSI Maps	Attractions
9	The Velvet Strand	Fingal	24	$2^{1}/_{2}$	Flat	Two-thirds on regional, remainder on third-class	50	Coast, Gardens, Bird sanctuary, Heritage
3	Fingal Circuit	Fingal, Meath	91	7	Hilly (in part)	Three-quarters on third-class, the remainder on regional	43, 50	Coast, Rolling countryside, Airport, some Heritage
6	Balrothery–Stamullin	Fingal, Meath	22	$1^{3}/_{4}$	Rolling (verging on)	Third-class	43	River, Bog, a little Heritage
14	Celbridge–Sallins	Kildare	51	5	Flat	Mainly on third-class, except for about 5 km on regional roads	49, 50	Butterfly farm, Steam museum, River, Canal, Heritage
15	Grand Canal System	Kildare	45	$4^{1}/_{2}$	Flat	Mostly third-class	49, 55	Canal, River, Woodland, some Heritage
16	Kilcock–Carbury	Kildare	61	6	Flat	Mainly third-class	49	Bog, Canal, Wildlife area, Woodland, Heritage
20	The Curragh of Kildare	Kildare	35	$4^{1}/_{4}$	Flat	Third-class except for 6 km on regional	55	Curragh plain, Gardens, Wildlife sanctuary, Equestrian centres, Heritage
18	Barrow Line	Kildare, Laois	47	$3^{1}/_{4}$	Flat	About half on regional, remainder on third-class except for 1.5 km on track and 4 km on N7	55	Canal, River, some Woodland, Heritage

A. Routes by County

No.	Name	County			Terrain	Road type	Map	Features
21	Royal Canal	Kildare, Meath	38	3¾	Flat	Half on regional and half on third-class	50	Rivers, Canal, Conservation area, Heritage
13	The Bog Circuit	Kildare, Offaly	95	7¼	Flat (mostly)	Mostly third-class	49, 55	Bog, Rivers, Canal, Heritage
17	Kilcullen-Castledermot	Kildare, Wicklow	74	7¼	Rolling	Third-class roads, except for about 4 km on regional and 3 km on national	55, 61	Rivers, Woodland, Scenic hills, Heritage
19	Hollywood Glen	Kildare, Wicklow	34	4	Hilly (verging on)	Mostly third-class	55, 56	Mountains, Glen, Forest, River, some Heritage
22	Abbey Road Tour	Louth	26	3	Hilly	Half on regional, remainder on third-class except for 2 km on busy N51	36, 43	River, Scenic hills, Heritage
23	Clogherhead	Louth	36	3½	Rolling	Two-thirds on regional, remainder on third-class	36, 43	Coast, River, Bird-watching, Heritage
24	Lugh's County	Louth	61	5¾	Rolling (verges on)	Three-quarters on third-class, the rest on regional	36	Coast, Mountain views, Heritage
25	Cooley Peninsula	Louth, Armagh	48	5¼	Hilly	Three-quarters on regional, remainder third-class except for 1 km on N1	36	Mountains, Forest, Lough, Coast, Heritage
11	Saints and Poets	Louth, Monaghan	67	6	Rolling	Three-quarters on third-class, remainder on regional	36	Pretty villages, Rivers, Bird sanctuary, Heritage

A. Routes by County

A. ROUTES BY COUNTY *contd*

No.	Name	County	Distance (km)	Time (hours)	Terrain	Roads	OSI Maps	Attractions
28	Ceanannas Mor	Meath, Westmeath	67	$5^3/_4$	Hilly at Loughcrew, otherwise rolling	Three-quarters on third-class, the rest on regional except for 2 km on N51 and N52	42	Scenic hills, Gardens, plenty of Heritage
10	Trim–Navan	Meath	57	6	Rolling	Mainly third-class	42	River, Woodland, plenty of Heritage
29	Hill of Tara	Meath	39	$4^1/_2$	Rolling	Mainly third-class except for 2-km stretch on N3	43	Scenic hills, Heritage
12	Holy Crosses and Haunted Castles	Meath, Fingal	40	$4^3/_4$	Rolling (mainly)	Third-class	43	Rolling countryside, Rivers, Haunted Castle, Heritage
26	Meath Coast	Meath, Louth	32	3	Flat	Mainly regional, some third-class, busy stretch on R132 (old N1) for 7 km	43	Coast, Rivers, Heritage
27	Valley of Kings	Meath, Louth	32	$4^1/_2$	Rolling mainly, hilly at Hill of Slane	Busy stretch on N51 for 3 km and N2 for 1 km, otherwise third-class roads	43	River, Ledwidge (poet) museum, plenty of Heritage
31	Blessington Lakes	Wicklow	31	$3^3/_4$	Rolling	Two-thirds on third-class, remainder on regional except for 1 km on N81	56	Mountains, Lake, Forest, Heritage

A. Routes by County

No.	Route	County	Distance	Time	Terrain	Roads	Page	Features
32	Sally Gap South	Wicklow	41–45	4½–5	Mountainous	Mainly quiet regional roads	56	Lakes, Mountains, Rivers, Waterfall, Woodland, a little Heritage
33	Ashford–Roundwood	Wicklow	28	2¾	Mountainous	Three-quarters regional, remainder on third-class	56	Lake, Mountains, River, Woodland, Gardens, a little Heritage
35	Sorrel Hill	Wicklow	25	2¾	Mountainous (a little)	Third-class	56	Lake, Mountains, Woodland, some Heritage
36	Trooperstown Hill and Glendalough	Wicklow	28	3½	Hilly	Third-class except for about 8 km on regional	56	Mountains, Woodland, Fishing, Heritage
37	Glencree Valley	Wicklow	28	3¼	Mountainous	Mainly third-class	56	Mountains, Woodland, Rivers, Waterfall, Gardens, Heritage
38	Ballykissangel	Wicklow	56	6	Hilly	Half on regional, remainder on third-class except for 1 km on N11	62	Mountains, Glen, River, Woodland, Coast, Heritage
39	Glenmalure and Aughrim	Wicklow	45	4½	Mountainous	Mainly third-class	56, 62	Mountains, Glen, Rivers, Fishing, Woodland, some Heritage
40	The Sugar Loafs	Wicklow, Dublin	30	4½	Mountainous	Half regional and half third-class	56	Mountains, Woodland, Garden, Coast, Heritage
30	Glen of Imaal	Wicklow	38	4½	Mountainous	Mainly third-class except for 3 km on regional and 3 km on the N81	55, 56, 61, 62	Mountains, Woodland, River, Heritage

B. Routes by Distance

No.	Name	County	Distance (km)	Time (hours)	Terrain	Roads	OSI Maps	Attractions
1	Fairy Castle Pub Crawl	Dublin	20	2½	Mountainous	Two-thirds on regional, the remaining on third-class. Busy stretch around Marlay Park. Route can be busy on weekends and holidays	50	Mountains, Woodland, a little Heritage, Old pubs
6	Balrothery–Stamullin	Fingal, Meath	22	1¾	Rolling (verging on)	Third-class	43	River, Bog, a little Heritage
9	The Velvet Strand	Fingal	24	2½	Flat	Two-thirds on regional, remainder on third-class	50	Coast, Gardens, Bird sanctuary, Heritage
5	Lambay Views	Fingal	25	2½	Hilly (verging on)	Two-thirds on third-class, the remainder on regional	43	Coastal views, Bird-watching, some Heritage
35	Sorrel Hill	Wicklow	25	2¾	Mountainous (a little)	Third-class	56	Lake, Mountains, Woodland, some Heritage
22	Abbey Road Tour	Louth	26	3	Hilly	Half on regional, remainder on third-class except for 2 km on busy N51	36, 43	River, Scenic hills, Heritage
33	Ashford–Roundwood	Wicklow	28	2¾	Mountainous	Three-quarters regional, remainder on third-class	56	Lake, Mountains, River, Woodland, Gardens, a little Heritage

B. Routes by Distance

No.	Name	County	Distance	Terrain	Road	Map	Features
36	Trooperstown Hill and Glendalough	Wicklow	28	3½	Hilly	Third-class except for about 8 km on regional	56	Mountains, Woodland, Fishing, Heritage
37	Glencree Valley	Wicklow	28	3¼	Mountainous	Mainly third-class	56	Mountains, Woodland, Rivers, Waterfall, Gardens, Heritage
4	Fair Fingal	Fingal	30	2½	Rolling (mainly)	Half third-class and half regional	43	Coast, Gardens, Windmills, Heritage
40	The Sugar Loafs	Wicklow, Dublin	30	4½	Mountainous	Half regional and half third-class	56	Mountains, Woodland, Garden, Coast, Heritage
31	Blessington Lakes	Wicklow	31	3¾	Rolling	Two-thirds on third-class, remainder on regional except for 1 km on N81	56	Mountains, Lake, Forest, Heritage
26	Meath Coast	Meath, Louth	32	3	Flat	Mainly regional, some third-class, busy stretch on R132 (old N1) for 7 km	43	Coast, Rivers, Heritage
27	Valley of Kings	Meath, Louth	32	4½	Rolling mainly, hilly at Hill of Slane	Busy stretch on N51 for 3 km and N2 for 1 km, otherwise third-class roads	43	River, Ledwidge (poet) museum, plenty of Heritage
19	Hollywood Glen	Kildare, Wicklow	34	4	Hilly (verging on)	Mostly third-class	55, 56	Mountains, Glen, Forest, River, some Heritage
20	The Curragh of Kildare	Kildare	35	4¼	Flat	Third-class except for 6 km on regional	55	Curragh plain, Gardens, Wildlife sanctuary, Equestrian centres, Heritage

B. Routes by Distance

B. Routes by Distance *contd*

No.	Name	County	Distance (km)	Time (hours)	Terrain	Roads	OSI Maps	Attractions
23	Clogherhead	Louth	36	$3^{1}/_{2}$	Rolling	Two-thirds on regional, remainder on third-class	36, 43	Coast, River, Bird-watching, Heritage
7	Bachall Iosa	Fingal	37	4	Hilly	All on regional except for 4 km on third-class	43	Rolling countryside, Music, Heritage
30	Glen of Imaal	Wicklow	38	$4^{1}/_{2}$	Mountainous	Mainly third-class except for 3 km on regional and 3 km on the N81	55, 56, 61, 62	Mountains, Woodland, River, Heritage
21	Royal Canal	Kildare, Meath	38	$3^{3}/_{4}$	Flat	Half on regional and half on third-class	50	Rivers, Canal, Conservation area, Heritage
29	Hill of Tara	Meath	39	$4^{1}/_{2}$	Rolling	Mainly third-class except for 2-km stretch on N3	43	Scenic hills, Heritage
12	Holy Crosses and Haunted Castles	Meath, Fingal	40	$4^{3}/_{4}$	Rolling (mainly)	Third-class	43	Rolling countryside, Rivers, Haunted Castle, Heritage
32	Sally Gap South	Wicklow	41-45	$4^{1}/_{2}$-5	Mountainous	Mainly quiet regional roads	56	Lakes, Mountains, Rivers, Waterfall, Woodland, a little Heritage
2	Brian Boru Circuit	Dublin, Fingal	44	5	Hilly (in part)	Three-quarters on cycle track, remainder on a mix of regional and third-class	50	Coast, Park, Wildlife sanctuary, Heritage

15	Grand Canal System	Kildare	4½	Flat	Mostly third-class	49, 55	Canal, River, Woodland, some Heritage
34	Sally Gap North	Dublin, Wicklow	4½	Mountainous	Three-quarters on regional, remainder on third-class	50, 56	Lakes, Mountains, Rivers, Woodland, a little Heritage
39	Glenmalure and Aughrim	Wicklow	4½	Mountainous	Mainly third-class	56, 62	Mountains, Glen, Rivers, Fishing, Woodland, some Heritage
18	Barrow Line	Kildare, Laois	3¼	Flat	About half on regional, remainder on third-class except for 1.5 km on track and 4 km on N7	55	Canal, River, some Woodland, Heritage
25	Cooley Peninsula	Louth, Armagh	5¼	Hilly	Three-quarters on regional, remainder third-class except for 1 km on N1	36	Mountains, Forest, Lough, Coast, Heritage
8	The Estuary Circuit	Fingal	5¼	Flat	Half regional and half third-class	43, 50	Coast, Park, Bird-watching, Heritage
14	Celbridge–Sallins	Kildare	5	Flat	Mainly on third-class, except for about 5 km on regional roads	49, 50	Butterfly farm, Steam museum, River, Canal, Heritage
38	Ballykissangel	Wicklow	6	Hilly	Half on regional, remainder on third-class except for 1 km on N11	62	Mountains, Glen, River, Woodland, Coast, Heritage
10	Trim–Navan	Meath	6	Rolling	Mainly third-class	42	River, Woodland, plenty of Heritage

B. Routes by Distance

B. Routes by Distance *contd*

No.	Name	County	Distance (km)	Time (hours)	Terrain	Roads	OSI Maps	Attractions
16	Kilcock–Carbury	Kildare	61	6	Flat	Mainly third-class	49	Bog, Canal, Wildlife area, Woodland, Heritage
24	Lugh's County	Louth	61	$5^3/4$	Rolling (verges on)	Three-quarters on third-class, the rest on regional	36	Coast, Mountain views, Heritage
11	Saints and Poets	Louth, Monaghan	67	6	Rolling	Three-quarters on third-class, remainder on regional	36	Pretty villages, Rivers, Bird sanctuary, Heritage
28	Ceanannas Mor	Meath, Westmeath	67	$5^3/4$	Hilly at Loughcrew, otherwise rolling	Three-quarters on third-class, the rest on regional except for 2 km on N51 and N52	42	Scenic hills, Gardens, plenty of Heritage
17	Kilcullen–Castledermot	Kildare, Wicklow	74	$7^1/4$	Rolling	Third-class roads, except for about 4 km on regional and 3 km on national	55, 61	Rivers, Woodland, Scenic hills, Heritage
3	Fingal Circuit	Fingal, Meath	91	7	Hilly (in part)	Three-quarters on third-class, the remainder on regional	43, 50	Coast, Rolling countryside, Airport, some Heritage
13	The Bog Circuit	Kildare, Offaly	95	$7^1/4$	Flat (mostly)	Mostly third-class	49, 55	Bog, Rivers, Canal, Heritage

C. Routes by Number

No.	Name	County	Distance (km)	Time (hours)	Terrain	Roads	OSI Maps	Attractions
1	Fairy Castle Pub Crawl	Dublin	20	2½	Mountainous	Two-thirds on regional, the remainder on third-class. Busy stretch around Marlay Park. Route can be busy on weekends and holidays	50	Mountains, Woodland, a little Heritage, Old pubs
2	Brian Boru Circuit	Dublin, Fingal	44	5	Hilly (in part)	Three-quarters on cycle track, remainder on a mix of regional and third-class	50	Coast, Park, Wildlife sanctuary, Heritage
3	Fingal Circuit	Fingal, Meath	91	7	Hilly (in part)	Three-quarters on third-class, the remainder on regional	43, 50	Coast, Rolling countryside, Airport, some Heritage
4	Fair Fingal	Fingal	30	2½	Rolling (mainly)	Half third-class and half regional	43	Coast, Gardens, Windmills, Heritage
5	Lambay Views	Fingal	25	2½	Hilly (verging on)	Two-thirds on third-class, the remainder on regional	43	Coastal views, Bird-watching, some Heritage
6	Balrothery–Stamullin	Fingal, Meath	22	1¾	Rolling (verging on)	Third-class	43	River, Bog, a little Heritage
7	Bachall Íosa	Fingal	37	4	Hilly	All on regional except for 4 km on third-class	43	Rolling countryside, Music, Heritage

C. Routes by Number

C. Routes by Number *contd*

No.	Name	County	Distance (km)	Time (hours)	Terrain	Roads	OSI Maps	Attractions
8	The Estuary Circuit	Fingal	50	$5^1/_4$	Flat	Half regional and half third-class	43, 50	Coast, Park, Bird-watching, Heritage
9	The Velvet Strand	Fingal	24	$2^1/_2$	Flat	Two-thirds on regional, remainder on third-class	50	Coast, Gardens, Bird sanctuary, Heritage
10	Trim–Navan	Meath	57	6	Rolling	Mainly third-class	42	River, Woodland, plenty of Heritage
11	Saints and Poets	Louth, Monaghan	67	6	Rolling	Three-quarters on third-class, remainder on regional	36	Pretty villages, Rivers, Bird sanctuary, Heritage
12	Holy Crosses and Haunted Castles	Meath, Fingal	40	$4^3/_4$	Rolling (mainly)	Third-class	43	Rolling countryside, Rivers, Haunted Castle, Heritage
13	The Bog Circuit	Kildare, Offaly	95	$7^1/_4$	Flat (mostly)	Mostly third-class	49, 55	Bog, Rivers, Canal, Heritage
14	Celbridge–Sallins	Kildare	51	5	Flat	Mainly on third-class, except for about 5 km on regional roads	49, 50	Butterfly farm, Steam museum, River, Canal, Heritage
15	Grand Canal System	Kildare	45	$4^1/_2$	Flat	Mostly third-class	49, 55	Canal, River, Woodland, some Heritage
16	Kilcock–Carbury	Kildare	61	6	Flat	Mainly third-class	49	Bog, Canal, Wildlife area, Woodland, Heritage

No.	Name	County			Terrain	Road type	Connections	Features
17	Kilcullen–Castledermot	Kildare, Wicklow	74	7¼	Rolling	Third-class roads, except for about 4 km on regional and 3 km on national	55, 61	Rivers, Woodland, Scenic hills, Heritage
18	Barrow Line	Kildare, Laois	47	3¼	Flat	About half on regional, remainder on third-class except for 1.5 km on track and 4 km on N7	55	Canal, River, some Woodland, Heritage
19	Hollywood Glen	Kildare, Wicklow	34	4	Hilly (verging on)	Mostly third-class	55, 56	Mountains, Glen, Forest, River, some Heritage
20	The Curragh of Kildare	Kildare	35	4¼	Flat	Third-class except for 6 km on regional	55	Curragh plain, Gardens, Wildlife sanctuary, Equestrian centres, Heritage
21	Royal Canal	Kildare, Meath	38	3¾	Flat	Half on regional and half on third-class	50	Rivers, Canal, Conservation area, Heritage
22	Abbey Road Tour	Louth	26	3	Hilly	Half on regional, remainder on third-class except for 2 km on busy N51	36, 43	River, Scenic hills, Heritage
23	Clogherhead	Louth	36	3½	Rolling	Two-thirds on regional, remainder on third-class	36, 43	Coast, River, Bird-watching, Heritage
24	Lugh's County	Louth	61	5¾	Rolling (verges on)	Three-quarters on third-class, the rest on regional	36	Coast, Mountain views, Heritage
25	Cooley Peninsula	Louth, Armagh	48	5¼	Hilly	Three-quarters on regional, remainder third-class except for 1 km on N1	36	Mountains, Forest, Lough, Coast, Heritage

C. Routes by Number *contd*

No.	Name	County	Distance (km)	Time (hours)	Terrain	Roads	OSI Maps	Attractions
26	Meath Coast	Meath, Louth	32	3	Flat	Mainly regional, some third-class, busy stretch on R132 (old N1) for 7 km	43	Coast, Rivers, Heritage
27	Valley of Kings	Meath, Louth	32	4½	Rolling mainly, hilly at Hill of Slane	Busy stretch on N51 for 3 km and N2 for 1 km, otherwise third-class roads	43	River, Ledwidge (poet) museum, plenty of Heritage
28	Ceanannas Mor	Meath, Westmeath	67	5¾	Hilly at Loughcrew, otherwise rolling	Three-quarters on third-class, the rest on regional except for 2 km on N51 and N52	42	Scenic hills, Gardens, plenty of Heritage
29	Hill of Tara	Meath	39	4½	Rolling	Mainly third-class except for 2-km stretch on N3	43	Scenic hills, Heritage
30	Glen of Imaal	Wicklow	38	4½	Mountainous	Mainly third-class except for 3 km on regional and 3 km on the N81	55, 56, 61, 62	Mountains, Woodland, River, Heritage
31	Blessington Lakes	Wicklow	31	3¾	Rolling	Two-thirds on third-class, remainder on regional except for 1 km on N81	56	Mountains, Lake, Forest, Heritage
32	Sally Gap South	Wicklow	41–45	4½–5	Mountainous	Mainly quiet regional roads	56	Lakes, Mountains, Rivers, Waterfall, Woodland, a little Heritage

No.	Name	Region			Terrain	Roads	Map	Features
33	Ashford–Roundwood	Wicklow	28	$2^{3}/_{4}$	Mountainous	Three-quarters regional, remainder on third-class	56	Lake, Mountains, River, Woodland, Gardens, a little Heritage
34	Sally Gap North	Dublin, Wicklow	45	$4^{1}/_{2}$	Mountainous	Three-quarters on regional, remainder on third-class	50, 56	Lakes, Mountains, Rivers, Woodland, a little Heritage
35	Sorrel Hill	Wicklow	25	$2^{3}/_{4}$	Mountainous (a little)	Third-class	56	Lake, Mountains, Woodland, some Heritage
36	Trooperstown Hill and Glendalough	Wicklow	28	$3^{1}/_{2}$	Hilly	Third-class except for about 8 km on regional	56	Mountains, Woodland, Fishing, Heritage
37	Glencree Valley	Wicklow	28	$3^{1}/_{4}$	Mountainous	Mainly third-class	56	Mountains, Woodland, Rivers, Waterfall, Gardens, Heritage
38	Ballykissangel	Wicklow	56	6	Hilly	Half on regional, remainder on third-class except for 1 km on N11	62	Mountains, Glen, River, Woodland, Coast, Heritage
39	Glenmalure and Aughrim	Wicklow	45	$4^{1}/_{2}$	Mountainous	Mainly third-class	56, 62	Mountains, Glen, Rivers, Fishing, Woodland, some Heritage
40	The Sugar Loafs	Wicklow, Dublin	30	$4^{1}/_{2}$	Mountainous	Half regional and half third-class	56	Mountains, Woodland, Garden, Coast, Heritage

D. Routes by Terrain

No.	Name	County	Distance (km)	Time (hours)	Terrain	Roads	OSI Maps	Attractions
8	The Estuary Circuit	Fingal	50	5¼	Flat	Half regional and half third-class	43, 50	Coast, Park, Bird-watching, Heritage
9	The Velvet Strand	Fingal	24	2½	Flat	Two-thirds on regional, remainder on third-class	50	Coast, Gardens, Bird sanctuary, Heritage
14	Celbridge–Sallins	Kildare	51	5	Flat	Mainly on third-class, except for about 5 km on regional roads	49, 50	Butterfly farm, Steam museum, River, Canal, Heritage
15	Grand Canal System	Kildare	45	4½	Flat	Mostly third-class	49, 55	Canal, River, Woodland, some Heritage
16	Kilcock–Carbury	Kildare	61	6	Flat	Mainly third-class	49	Bog, Canal, Wildlife area, Woodland, Heritage
18	Barrow Line	Kildare, Laois	47	3¼	Flat	About half on regional, remainder on third-class except for 1.5 km on track and 4 km on N7	55	Canal, River, some Woodland, Heritage
20	The Curragh of Kildare	Kildare	35	4¼	Flat	Third-class except for 6 km on regional	55	Curragh plain, Gardens, Wildlife sanctuary, Equestrian centres, Heritage

D. Routes by Terrain

No.	Route	Counties			Terrain	Roads		Features
21	Royal Canal	Kildare, Meath	38	3¾	Flat	Half on regional and half on third-class	50	Rivers, Canal, Conservation area, Heritage
26	Meath Coast	Meath, Louth	32	3	Flat	Mainly regional, some third-class, busy stretch on R132 (old N1) for 7 km	43	Coast, Rivers, Heritage
13	The Bog Circuit	Kildare, Offaly	95	7¼	Flat (mostly)	Mostly third-class	49, 55	Bog, Rivers, Canal, Heritage
7	Bachall Iosa	Fingal	37	4	Hilly	All on regional except for 4 km on third-class	43	Rolling countryside, Music, Heritage
22	Abbey Road Tour	Louth	26	3	Hilly	Half on regional, remainder on third-class except for 2 km on busy N51	36, 43	River, Scenic hills, Heritage
25	Cooley Peninsula	Louth, Armagh	48	5¼	Hilly	Three-quarters on regional, remainder third-class except for 1 km on N1	36	Mountains, Forest, Lough, Coast, Heritage
36	Trooperstown Hill and Glendalough	Wicklow	28	3½	Hilly	Third-class except for about 8 km on regional	56	Mountains, Woodland, Fishing, Heritage
38	Ballykissangel	Wicklow	56	6	Hilly	Half on regional, remainder on third-class except for 1 km on N11	62	Mountains, Glen, River, Woodland, Coast, Heritage
19	Hollywood Glen	Kildare, Wicklow	34	4	Hilly (verging on)	Mostly third-class	55, 56	Mountains, Glen, Forest, River, some Heritage

D. Routes by Terrain

D. ROUTES BY TERRAIN *contd*

No.	Name	County	Distance (km)	Time (hours)	Terrain	Roads	OSI Maps	Attractions
2	Brian Boru Circuit	Dublin, Fingal	44	5	Hilly (in part)	Three-quarters on cycle track, remainder on a mix of regional and third-class	50	Coast, Park, Wildlife sanctuary, Heritage
3	Fingal Circuit	Fingal, Meath	91	7	Hilly (in part)	Three-quarters on third-class, the remainder on regional	43, 50	Coast, Rolling country-side, Airport, some Heritage
5	Lambay Views	Fingal	25	2½	Hilly (verging on)	Two-thirds on third-class, the remainder on regional	43	Coastal views, Bird-watching, some Heritage
28	Ceanannas Mor	Meath, Westmeath	67	5¾	Hilly at Loughcrew, otherwise rolling	Three-quarters on third-class, the rest on regional except for 2 km on N51 and N52	42	Scenic hills, Gardens, plenty of Heritage
1	Fairy Castle Pub Crawl	Dublin	20	2½	Mountainous	Two-thirds on regional, the remaining on third-class. Busy stretch around Marlay Park. Route can be busy on weekends and holidays	50	Mountains, Woodland, a little Heritage, Old pubs
30	Glen of Imaal	Wicklow	38	4½	Mountainous	Mainly third-class except for 3 km on regional and 3 km on the N81	55, 56, 61, 62	Mountains, Woodland, River, Heritage

D. Routes by Terrain

No.	Name	County			Terrain	Roads	Map	Features
32	Sally Gap South	Wicklow	41-45	4½-5	Mountainous	Mainly quiet regional roads	56	Lakes, Mountains, Rivers, Waterfall, Woodland, a little Heritage
33	Ashford-Roundwood	Wicklow	28	2¾	Mountainous	Three-quarters regional, remainder on third-class	56	Lake, Mountains, River, Woodland, Gardens, a little Heritage
34	Sally Gap North	Dublin, Wicklow	45	4½	Mountainous	Three-quarters on regional, remainder on third-class	50, 56	Lakes, Mountains, Rivers, Woodland, a little Heritage
37	Glencree Valley	Wicklow	28	3¼	Mountainous	Mainly third-class	56	Mountains, Woodland, Rivers, Waterfall, Gardens, Heritage
39	Glenmalure and Aughrim	Wicklow	45	4½	Mountainous	Mainly third-class	56, 62	Mountains, Glen, Rivers, Fishing, Woodland, some Heritage
40	The Sugar Loafs	Wicklow, Dublin	30	4½	Mountainous	Half regional and half third-class	56	Mountains, Woodland, Garden, Coast, Heritage
35	Sorrel Hill	Wicklow	25	2¾	Mountainous (a little)	Third-class	56	Lake, Mountains, Woodland, some Heritage
10	Trim-Navan	Meath	57	6	Rolling	Mainly third-class	42	River, Woodland, plenty of Heritage
11	Saints and Poets	Louth, Monaghan	67	6	Rolling	Three-quarters on third-class, remainder on regional	36	Pretty villages, Rivers, Bird sanctuary, Heritage

D. Routes by Terrain

D. ROUTES BY TERRAIN contd

No.	Name	County	Distance (km)	Time (hours)	Terrain	Roads	OSI Maps	Attractions
17	Kilcullen–Castledermot	Kildare, Wicklow	74	7¼	Rolling	Third-class roads, except for about 4 km on regional and 3 km on national	55, 61	Rivers, Woodland, Scenic hills, Heritage
23	Clogherhead	Louth	36	3½	Rolling	Two-thirds on regional, remainder on third-class	36, 43	Coast, River, Bird-watching, Heritage
29	Hill of Tara	Meath	39	4½	Rolling	Mainly third-class except for 2-km stretch on N3	43	Scenic hills, Heritage
31	Blessington Lakes	Wicklow	31	3¾	Rolling	Two-thirds on third-class, remainder on regional except for 1 km on N81	56	Mountains, Lake, Forest, Heritage
4	Fair Fingal	Fingal	30	2½	Rolling (mainly)	Half third-class and half regional	43	Coast, Gardens, Windmills, Heritage
12	Holy Crosses and Haunted Castles	Meath, Fingal	40	4¾	Rolling (mainly)	Third-class	43	Rolling countryside, Rivers, Haunted Castle, Heritage
24	Lugh's County	Louth	61	5¾	Rolling (verges on)	Three-quarters on third-class, the rest on regional	36	Coast, Mountain views, Heritage
6	Balrothery–Stamullin	Fingal, Meath	22	1¾	Rolling (verging on)	Third-class	43	River, Bog, a little Heritage
27	Valley of Kings	Meath, Louth	32	4½	Rolling mainly, hilly at Hill of Slane	Busy stretch on N51 for 3 km and N2 for 1 km, otherwise third-class roads	43	River, Ledwidge (poet) museum, plenty of Heritage

Bibliography

Miscellaneous

Cabot, David, *Irish Birds*, Collins, 2004
Joyce, Dan, Carlton Reid & Paul Vincent, *The Complete Book of Cycling*, Chancellor Press, 2000
Sterry, Paul & Derek Mooney, *Complete Irish Wildlife*, Harper Collins, 2004

Local History

Archer, Patrick, *Fair Fingal*, An Taisce, Fingal, 1975
Automobile Association, *Illustrated Road Book of Ireland*, 1970
Balbriggan: A History for the Millennium, Balbriggan and District Historical Society, 1999
Bates, Peadar, *Donabate and Portrane — a history*, 2001
Carty, Mary-Rose, *History of Killeen Castle*, Carty/Lynch, 1991
Costello, Con, *Guide to Kildare and West Wicklow*, Leinster Leader, 2001
Costello, Con, *Kildare Saints, Scholars and Horses 1991*, Leinster Leader, 1991
Fewer, Michael, *By Swerve of Shore — Exploring Dublin's Coast*, Gill & Macmillan, 2002
Flynn, Arthur & Jim Brophy, *The Book of Wicklow — Towns and Villages in the Garden of Ireland*, Kestrel Books, 1999
From the Nanny to the Boyne, A Local History, Meath East Co-operative Society Ltd, *c.* 1999
Lalor, Brian, *Dublin Bay from Killiney to Howth*, O'Brien Press, 1990
Old Tales of Fingal, compiled by An Taisce Fingal, 1984
Olden Times in Garristown, Garristown Historical Society, 2000
Slevin, Michael, *The Book of Tara*, Irish American Book Co., 1997
Wren, Jimmy, *The Villages of Dublin*, Tomar Publications, 1987

SOME INTERNET SITES

http://www.irishrail.ie	Rail information
https://www.buseireann.ie/	Bus information
http://www.meteireann.ie	Weather forecast
http://www.ctc.org.uk/	Tips on cycling
http://www.nsc.ie/RoadSafety/	Road safety
http://www.iwt.ie/	Information on Irish wildlife
http://www.birdwatchireland.ie/	Information on Irish birds
http://www.rte.ie/radio/	
mooneygoeswild//	Information on Irish wildlife
http://www.coilte.ie/	Forestry
http://www.ipcc.ie/	Information on bogs
http://www.irelandseye.com/	Irish history and culture
http://www.ireland.ie/	Irish towns and villages
http://www.heritageireland.ie/	Heritage sites in Ireland
http://www.countywicklow.com/	Wicklow heritage
http://www.meathtourism.ie/	Meath heritage
http://www.louthonline.com/	History of Louth
http://kildare.ie/local-history/	
kildare.htm	History of Kildare
http://www.fingalcoco.ie	Heritage sites in Fingal